work this way

BRUCE TULGAN

work this way

INVENTING YOUR CAREER IN THE WORKPLACE OF THE FUTURE

CAPSTONE

This edition first published 1998
Capstone Publishing Limited
Oxford Centre for Innovation
Mill Street
Oxford OX2 0JX
United Kingdom

First published by Hyperion, New York

British Library Cataloguing in Publication Data
A CIP catalogue record for this book is available from the British Library

ISBN 1–900961–563

Designed and typeset by Forewords, Oxford
Printed and bound by T.J. Press Ltd, Padstow, Cornwall

This book is printed on acid-free paper

Contents

Dedication
This book is dedicated to Debby Applegate.

Acknowledgements

I want to thank all the people – more than a thousand now – whom I've interviewed in the last four years. You are my greatest teachers and my work is driven by your collective brilliance.

Special thanks to the following interviewees: Bela Barner, Kim Coombs, David Hickman, Maia Gahtan, Paige Green, Ron Green, Ben Grinnell, Nicolette Harkins, Ingrid Honaker, Heather Lamm, Sandra Luckow, Maria Ricciardone, Brian Rod, and Aaron Rulnick.

To all those I've met along the way in all the companies, associations, and schools where I've been so fortunate to speak: thank you for taking the time to be in my audience. I am honored by your kindness.

I am blessed with many dear friends and I feel I owe you all my deepest gratitude.

To my cohorts at Rainmaker, Inc., past and present, thank you for joining me in studying our generation's experience in the workplace, especially Mark Kurber, Heather Boardman, Ruth Gutman, Jeff Katz, Homer Robinson, and Soyong Cho. I owe much to Jeff Coombs, who is the other managing principal at Rainmaker. Since you joined Rainmaker, Jeff, you have expressed great faith in me and I want you to know that I have 100 percent faith in you. How can I thank you enough for all of your hard work and commitment? Jeff is my alter ego in this enterprise. Without Jeff, there would be no such thing as Rainmaker, Inc. Jeff is also the kindest and most sincere person I have ever known – and a true friend.

I came to write this book with Hyperion through a sequence of coincidences: Lou Cove asked me to write a series of columns, which led to a series I wrote for Tripod on-line. Editor extraordinaire Lisa Jenner Hudson read my series on Tripod and asked if I would be interested in writing a book. Hours after I first met with Lisa, Lou Cove was introducing me to agent extraordinaire Bob Levine, who made the deal with Lisa. Thus, I owe great thanks to Lou Cove.

To Lisa Jenner Hudson: early on, Lisa moved me in a fundamentally different direction than that which I first intended, and in so doing, she helped shape the nature of the book. Since then, she has added value every step of the way with her effective but gentle edits. Lisa: you are destined for greatness as an editor. I am very grateful for your influence, for the the ease with which we have worked together, and for your friendship. I am also grateful to Lisa for giving me the chance to work with Hyperion, a vibrant publishing house with an impressive list of books – I am honored to be in such great company.

Then there's Bob Levine. If I had sat alone in a room and dreamed up the perfect literary agent, I couldn't have dreamed an agent as perfect as Bob – he is a godsend. He has my total and complete confidence, and I feel very lucky to have my career in his hands. Bob: thank you so much for representing me. Also, thanks to Conrad Rippy, Esq., Bob's associate who worked so hard on the contract, and to Bob's assistant Paula Marsili, who was so nice to me.

I want to give special thanks to my entire family. To my brother Jim, sister Ronna, sister-in-law Terri, brother-in-law Tom; my nieces Elisa, Perry, and Erin and my nephew Joey; my grandmother Gertrude; my in-laws the Applegates, Julie, Paul, Shan, and Tanya; my parents Norma and Henry; and my wife Debby Applegate: Thank you (again) for being the greatest family in the world. I love you all very much.

In very special thanks to my parents: Thanks for inventing me, raising me, believing in me, and giving me so much to believe in.

To my wife Debby Applegate, who is the greatest miracle of

fate: it is so hard for me to identify the boundaries between my thoughts and yours, my feelings and yours, my creative expressions and yours. Where do you end and I begin? Everything I do is in collaboration with you, Debby, because our life together is a collaboration. I hope someday to die in your arms.

About the author

Bruce Tulgan is the founder of Rainmaker, Inc., a think tank which researches the working lives of Americans born between 1963 and 1977. He has been a featured speaker to business leaders, managers, association members, young workers, and students all over North America and even abroad. Bruce's first book, *Managing Generation X: How to Bring Out the Best in Young Talent* (Merritt, 1995), is a guide to managing young rising stars in the workplace. His writing has appeared in the New York Times and the Los Angeles Times, as well as numerous other newspapers, magazines, professional journals, on-line sources and academic publications. His work has been the subject of scores of news articles across the country and news reports on radio and television programs. While Bruce retired from the practice of law in 1994, he is still admitted to the bar in New York and Massachusetts. He has taught management on the graduate level as an Assistant Professor of Management and holds a fourth degree black belt in Uechi Ryu Karate. Bruce lives with his wife Debby Applegate in New Haven, Connecticut.

Executive summary

Memo

TO: The workforce of the future

FROM: Bruce Tulgan

RE: *Work This Way*

1. The job as we have known it is coming to an end

(a) There are six symptoms of the job's demise.

> ▷ Permanent downsizing.
> ▷ Declining relative wages.
> ▷ Underutilization of skilled labor.
> ▷ Rise of temporary employment.
> ▷ Employee leasing.
> ▷ Wave of small business start-ups.

(b) There are seven forces shaping the 'post-jobs era.'

> ▷ Reengineering.
> ▷ Restructuring.
> ▷ Technology.
> ▷ Knowledge work.
> ▷ Diversity.
> ▷ Globalization.
> ▷ The virtual workplace.

(c) When it comes to designing our careers in the workplace of the future, we are on our own.

2. Welcome to the post-jobs era, where change equals opportunity

  ▷ Sell your most valuable talents on the open market.
  ▷ If you are working in a job which does not let you maximize your abilities, take on an additional project that you feel **is** worthy of you.
  ▷ If you are temping, use the experience to practice adapting quickly; to scout out further opportunities; build relationships; and start racking up achievements which prove your ability to add value.
  ▷ Consider starting your own business.
  ▷ Be flexible and ready to adapt to new roles wherever you are.
  ▷ Reinvent the meaning of 'support staff.'
  ▷ Initiate a plan for continuous learning.
  ▷ Leverage your uniqueness.
  ▷ Globalize yourself.
  ▷ Become a virtual worker extraordinaire.

3. Learn voraciously

(a) Two key skills to master:

  ▷ Multiple focus.
  ▷ Selective elimination.

(b) Create your own opportunities to learn:

  ▷ Take control of your college experience.
  ▷ Turn paraprofessional jobs into apprenticeships.
  ▷ Take control of your graduate school experience.
  ▷ Maximize all corporate training opportunities.
  ▷ Don't let obstacles stand in your way.
  ▷ Turn everday life into a learning lab.

4. Learn what you love

(a) Anything you learn is marketable, so learn what you love.

> ▷ If you don't know what you love to learn, keep a journal of your spontaneous learning and find out.

(b) In everything you do, practice these key transferable skills ('the core curriculum for the post-jobs era'):

> ▷ Focus on results.
> ▷ Adapt to new situations quickly.
> ▷ Manage information.
> ▷ Think critically.
> ▷ Define and redefine and solve problems.
> ▷ Communicate well and relate to people.
> ▷ Become a great team player.
> ▷ Negotiate and resolve conflicts.
> ▷ Master foreign languages and foreign cultures.
> ▷ Gain computer and Internet competence.
> ▷ Do what matters most to you.

5. Get beyond networking

(a) Invest in relationships with individuals, because such relationships will be the most reliable institutions in the post-jobs era.

(b) Formulate strategies to connect with people who can help you:

> ▷ Frame relationships in terms of what you have to offer.
> ▷ Identify and seek out the right decision makers.
> ▷ Turn every contact into a multiple contact.
> ▷ Do research before making contact.
> ▷ Use a mutual connection if you have one.
> ▷ Make your communiqués interesting and useful.

    ▷ Identify and win over gatekeepers.

    ▷ Once you get on the radar screen, prove that you are more than a blip.

    ▷ Become Ms or Mr Follow-Up.

    ▷ Keep your contact information up to date and keep others up to date with your current contact information.

    ▷ Take personal responsibility for maintaining the positive energy in relationships.

6. Maximize relationship opportunities

    ▷ Don't be afraid to ask family and friends for help.

    ▷ Volunteer to work with others on a shared goal.

    ▷ Bring together people with mutual interests.

    ▷ Give subordinates the power to excel.

    ▷ Manage your boss in a way that gives you room to excel.

    ▷ Develop a total customer service mindset.

    ▷ Become a great customer.

    ▷ Be the diligent protege of a worthy mentor.

    ▷ Be a mentor.

7. Become a day-to-day value adder

(a) There are five different ways to add value:

    ▷ Identify a problem that others have not yet identified.

    ▷ Solve a problem that others have not yet solved.

    ▷ Invent a brand new service or product.

    ▷ Improve an existing service or product.

    ▷ Deliver an existing service or product in a timely, competent manner.

(b) Follow seven steps to sell your added value.

▷ Define the value for yourself.
▷ Create an effective sales message to persuade the right decision makers.
▷ Deliver the message.
▷ Close the deal.
▷ Add the value you promised to add and always go the extra mile.
▷ Get paid.
▷ Provide follow-up service.

(c) Here are ten opportunities to be a day-to-day value adder.

▷ Just-a-jobbing.
▷ Fast tracking.
▷ Reinventing your role in any organization.
▷ Leaving without really leaving.
▷ Effective job juggling.
▷ Job hopping.
▷ Entrepreneuring.
▷ Knowledge working.
▷ Volunteering for community service.
▷ Feathering your nest.

8. Keep moving your life toward balance.

(a) In a profoundly insecure world, we owe it to ourselves to be our own greatest source of security.

(b) Six values and priorities to guide you.

▷ Quality.
▷ Integrity.
▷ Fulfillment (reach for the stars).
▷ Well-being (mind, body, and spirit).
▷ Connection with others.
▷ Personal growth.

(c) Seize daily opportunities to add balance in your life.

> ▷ Gain control of your creative space.
> ▷ Give your mind a treat.
> ▷ Give your body a treat.
> ▷ Believe in something.
> ▷ Spend time with people you care about.
> ▷ Gain control of your time.

9. Take it one year at a time

(a) A long-term goal is like a mirage in the desert. It's a useful hallucination if it keeps moving you in the right direction, but you'll probably never reach the oasis.

(b) Make a one year plan.

> ▷ Set one year goals for learning, relationships, adding value, and moving your life toward balance.
> ▷ Map out all the intermediate goals and deadlines along the way to each one year goal.
> ▷ Carve up the achievement of each intermediate goal into bite sized chunks, which can be accomplished in less than a day (daily actions).
> ▷ Schedule your time effectively to plan all the daily actions necessary to achieve your goals.
> ▷ Monitor feedback from the world around you and continue making necessary adjustments in your goals and plans every step of the way.

Introduction

I was a lawyer for 428 days, and then, three years ago, at the age of twenty-six, I retired.

After going straight through seventeen years of school (because my parents didn't think it was a good idea to take time off) and then choosing exactly the kind of job my parents thought I should have, I was frustrated and bored. It seemed to me the career path I was trying to follow was obsolete.

I was also struck by the fact that the senior lawyers in the law firm didn't have a clue about how to manage people my age or what was at stake for us in our careers. As I talked with more and more people my age, I could see there was a widespread generation gap in the workplace. I decided to write a book that would narrow that gap, and I called it *Managing Generation X*.

In writing *Managing Generation X*, I wanted to turn the 'slacker' stereotype on its head and change the meaning of 'Generation X.' I wanted to let managers know what young people in the workplace are thinking about our work and our careers, show managers what is working and what isn't, and teach managers how to bring out the best in young people.

I based *Managing Generation X* on in-depth interviews with people in their twenties who are trying to succeed in today's rapidly changing workplace. I asked them how they were being managed, how it affected their work, how they wanted to be managed, and how they looked at their work and their careers. Most were very pleased to have a chance to tell managers how they would like to be treated. Others had horror stories. Out of these interviews came terrific, practical, common-sense recommendations for improving the working lives of people our age and for those who manage us.

These interviews were such an incredible learning experience that I wanted to keep doing them, even after I finished the book. So I founded a small think tank, Rainmaker, Inc., to continue studying the experience of our generation in the workplace. Our message was simple: 'Xers are not slackers! Xers are the workforce of the future.' And that message seemed to catch on. We started getting some attention from the news media, which led to speaking engagements, and we have been in the 'workforce of the future' business ever since. I have been lucky enough to speak to thousands of managers, business leaders, association members, students, and young workers at meetings, conferences, and campuses all over the United States and Canada (and even overseas) about how the radical changes in today's workplace are affecting our generation.

As I was giving speeches intended for people in their forties, fifties, and sixties, I could usually see a handful of people closer to my own age in the audience. That made me a little nervous because I was making a living as a 'spokesperson' for our generation and I was afraid some of these Xers were going to raise their hands and say, 'Hey, I'm twenty-five and you're full of shit.' But they didn't. Instead, they started coming up to me after I was done speaking and saying stuff like, 'Hey, I'm twenty-five and you just described my life,' or 'That's exactly where I am coming from,' or 'I've had a lot of those experiences too.'

They also would come up to me and ask for my advice about how they should manage their careers. At first, the best I could do was commiserate with them about how tough it is to be starting a career in today's economy. We talked about the disappearance of the old-fashioned workplace bargain – where you would pay your dues and climb the ladder and have job security and then retire with a pension. We talked about how so many people our age are stuck in temp jobs or retail jobs or otherwise underemployed, and how we all have friends who have had to move back with their parents for a while after college. We talked about all the people our age who do have jobs and how they have to prove themselves every single day just to stay afloat. We had a lot to talk about.

These conversations inspired me to refocus my research. I started asking my interviewees less about how they are being managed and more about how they are managing themselves. What strategies are working for people our age out there in the real world?

I also started to look more closely at what I was learning from all the business leaders I've been meeting: while many are digging in their heels and resisting change, many more are convinced that the economy is going through a radical transformation that is changing the nature of work forever. Reengineering, restructuring, and downsizing are not merely upheavals in the system which will eventually pass. These changes are fundamentally reshaping the relationship between employers and employees, forever.

All of a sudden, it hit me. I realized that it's all over. Not just job security, I mean jobs are all over. We have entered what I call 'the post-jobs era,' and there is no turning back.

Scary? Yes, but don't be alarmed. There is tremendous opportunity in all of these changes, especially for people who are not stuck in the workplace of the past – or committed to obsolete career paths. This is how, I believe, our generation can level the career playing field: most of us would never dream of building a career around a long-term affiliation with one established company. Those of our generation have always known that the only success and security we will ever have is that which we build from within ourselves. This expectation, in and of itself, makes us uniquely suited to thrive in the post-jobs era.

But, wait. There's more.

Look at the trends shaping the future: (1) unstable institutions; (2) self-reliant individuals; (3) the tidal wave of information and technology; and (4) the continuing acceleration of the pace of change. Aren't you already in tune with these trends? Look within yourself: Are you cautious when dealing with established institutions? Flexible? Adaptable? Fiercely independent? Comfortable with information and technology? Creative? Always monitoring your surroundings? Looking for fast feedback from the world around you? Trying to gauge what's changing and what is staying the same?

Our generation is shaped by the very same trends shaping the future – the same forces shaping the post-jobs era. The career paths ahead look nothing like the career paths our parents traveled. Most of us wouldn't want the kinds of careers our parents had anyway.

Those of our generation are pioneers of a whole new career paradigm. Our careers are not anchored to any one job or any one company or any one industry. We are moving around a lot, from one new experience to the other, building ourselves with each new experience, creating a new kind of security and success from within ourselves. And while practically all of us are discovering that the old career paths are washed out, many are finding new career paths which are leading us on exciting new journeys. I hope that reading about those journeys will inspire you and give you some great ideas about how to design your own.

Through my interviews, I have sought answers to the questions many of us have asked ourselves: What strategies are working out there? How do you turn temp jobs and retail jobs into great career opportunities? How do you turn job-hopping into a positive? How do you start your own company without much money? What's the difference these days between working for someone else and working for yourself? How do you make sure to keep building your skills? How do you cultivate relationships with people who can help you? How do you spot opportunities to add value and then market yourself into those creative challenges? How do you succeed and still keep the rest of your life in balance? How can you make a career plan when everything around you is changing so fast?

I have unearthed some affective new strategies which people our age are using to navigate our way around obstacles to success (or over them, or under them, or straight through them). A lot of young people are doing pretty well out there in the thick of this changing economy. Very few have all the answers. Most are running into plenty of dead-ends. But, we are also regrouping and trying again... often, several times over. We are creating self-designed, self-managed careers. And, we are discovering a lot of new career strategies that work in the post-jobs era.

Sharing those strategies is what this book is all about.

In Chapters 1 and 2, I will introduce you to the post-jobs era and also to some of the people among the more than 1,000 I've interviewed. Throughout this book, I have let some of my most impressive interviewees speak to you in their own voices; of their own experiences and strategies for today's world.

The rest of this book is designed to help you let go of the workplace of the past and the old-fashioned concept of a 'job' (working in the same company or the same industry for decades, paying your dues, climbing the ladder). That approach may have worked for your parents in the past, but it's probably not working for them now, and it's definitely not going to work for you.

I've organized the remaining chapters into the five common denominators I found among my interviewees who are reinventing success in the post-jobs era:

1. *Voracious learning:* Turn every experience into an opportunity to build skills, knowledge, and wisdom that you can sell.

2. *Relationships:* Cultivate authentic bonds with people who can help you.

3. *Day-to-day value adding:* Seize opportunities to add value wherever you can find them – identify and solve problems; invent or improve products and services; deliver products (or perform services) faster, smarter, better, or cheaper.

4. *Moving yourself toward balance:* Set clear priorities in your

working life and your personal life – health, exercise, family, fun – and live by them no matter what anyone says.

5.   *Planning, one year at a time:* Establish clear long-term goals, but not because they will have anything to do with where you end up in the long term. Long-term goals will help you make good decisions right now and make the best use of your time every day. But it's just as important to monitor the feedback you are getting from the world around you and always be ready to stop, revise your plans, adjust your position, and start moving in a new direction.

As you let go of the workplace of the past and move forward into the post-jobs era, bring this book along with you. Chances are that you will recognize some of the strategies as ones you are already using. My hope is that you will also find a lot of new strategies that you can start using right away to design your own self-managed career and increase your personal power in the post-jobs era.

The end of the job as we know it . . .

Chapter 1

❝ I am stuck working as a sales clerk in a clothing store and I don't even have enough hours here. I don't have benefits and every week I have to fight for hours. I can't even afford to live on my own, so I am stuck in the same room I lived in before I went to college. Which is another thing. . . . This makes me really glad I spent four years in college. It's bullshit.

Sales clerk, retail clothing store, twenty-three

❝ I'm about to graduate with my Ph.D. from one of the top institutions in this country and I am being told that there are 800 applicants for every available position. I know a bunch of people who have been on the market for several years, without getting the kind of job they were trained for. . . . Some go from one part time job to another, filling in for professors who are on sabbaticals or whatever. Some are just getting fed up and leaving academics, which is pretty hard after working for seven years to get a doctorate. . . . It's ridiculous.

Ph.D. candidate, twenty-eight

❝ I majored in social work as an undergraduate, but there are just no jobs in my major. Some people are telling me to go into an MSW program. . . . But, how do I know that there will be a job on the other end of that? Then some people are telling me that what you major in doesn't matter at all. So I wish I had majored in something a little less specific. Right now, I am working two part-time jobs that I don't hate, but I am going to have to get another part-time job if I can't get more hours in the ones I already have.

Recent college graduate, twenty-two

❝ I graduated from law school almost four years ago. I started in a big firm in New York [and] was there for less than two years. . . . I left to go to a firm that was more cutting edge in terms of the work that was being done [and] in terms of . . . managing young lawyers. . . . Less than a year later, I jumped ship again and I'm going to my fourth law firm job in less than four years. But, that is just the way it is these days, and it just makes sense for me to do it. Who knows? By this time next year, I may not even be a lawyer anymore.

Lawyer, twenty-nine

❝ I got myself in the door for an interview but these guys were really hard-assed about it. . . . I was trying to negotiate with them and . . . convince them that, even though I didn't have a lot of experience. . . . I was a really hard worker, that I learn fast, that I would be glad to prove myself. . . . They told me they would give me a chance, but I would have to work for free on a trial basis for a while. They didn't even say for how long. . . . They said they would give me a chance to get my foot in the door. . . . I thought they were kidding. Believe me, they weren't. I did it and figured at least I would be able to get some experience in the management consulting world, which I was really interested in. After about five weeks. . . . I said, 'Screw this,' and quit.

Management consultant, formerly juggled several part-time jobs, currently unemployed, twenty-six

❝ I was going to work every day thinking, 'Man, if I don't prove my value today, I could be out of a job.' Every day I have to be selling myself. And I've only got one customer – my boss. I've been thinking lately, if I start my own company, I'm not taking such a big risk. I'll be diversifying my risk because, even if I have to be selling every day, at least I'll have more than one customer.

Software developer, would-be entrepreneur, twenty-six

❝ I passed the bar exam in two states and I can't find a job as a lawyer. For a while, I had to move back in with my mum and just try to figure out what to do. Finally, I ended up getting a job with a paralegal temp agency and doing paralegal work. Luckily . . . one of the lawyers at the place I got assigned offered me something a little more like lawyer work. But, they also knew they could get me for next to nothing. I actually made less working as a lawyer for a while than I was making as a paralegal. But at least I got my foot in the door.

Lawyer, twenty-eight

> ❝ It's hard to find a job that's a good match with my inter-
> ests and my skills. I'm working as a temp to pay the bills.
> Right now I have to live modestly, lower my expectations a
> little, and keep my eyes open for the right opportunity.
> Most of my creative energy goes into a software program
> I am trying to develop on my own, when I have time. I've
> learned a lot doing it, and I've thought about trying to
> create my own business around it. Everyone can't be Bill
> Gates. But maybe I'm learning something that a guy like
> Gates would find valuable in an employee.
>
> *Temporary employee, twenty-four*

■ What's going on?

If you are in the early stages of your career, you may have
noticed that there is definitely something weird going on out
there. All the entry-level jobs, for which we've supposedly
been in training for the last twenty years, seem to have
disappeared while we were busy growing up. Our training
never veered too far from the traditional path – we went to
school, participated in some extracurricular activities, maybe
worked in a few internships. That should have been enough
to give us a running start down the traditional career path, as
long as the day-to-day working world turned out to be
something like we've been taught to expect it would be.
Here's the thing: virtually everything we have been taught to
expect from the day-to-day working world is pretty much
obsolete. You see, the old-fashioned job, as we once knew it,
has come to an end.

■ The end of the job as we once knew it

For more than fifty years, most people worked in an
environment dominated by large organizations with clear
corporate ladders one could expect to climb over the course of
a twenty- or thirty-year career. Most employment relationships were long-term, if not lifelong. If you gave your loyalty,
talent and hard work to the right company, you would be

rewarded with a lifelong job in the company and then retirement with a decent pension.

Work was arranged in neat little packages called 'jobs.' You could expect a 'job description' to set boundaries around your work and define the specific tasks you were supposed to do – not just so you could tell exactly what was 'your job,' but also so you could tell what was 'not your job' and, therefore, not your problem. Most of your formal training occurred in school, before you entered the workforce. Once you got a job, you learned the specific things you needed to learn to be able to do 'your job.' You worked in the same building every day, answered to one boss, probably the next guy up the company ladder. You did what your boss told you to do for about eight hours a day (sometimes a little more, sometimes a little less) and then you went home for dinner.

These careers were linear: you started with an 'entry level' job and moved along from one pay raise to the next, from one middle management position to the next – if your boss got promoted, maybe you would get his job and then probably keep it, until he got promoted again – and so on. In the workplace of the past, seniority was very, very important: the longer you worked in a particular company, the more seniority you accumulated – and the more seniority you had, the more status, power, and salary you could expect. For those in the workforce of the past, it made a lot of sense to get a good 'job' in a good company and stay there – pay your dues, climb the ladder and become part of the club.

The problem is, *there is no club anymore* because there is no such thing anymore as a good old-fashioned 'job.' In today's economy, there are six obvious symptoms of the job's demise:

> ▷ Permanent downsizing
> ▷ Declining relative wages
> ▷ Underutilization of skilled labor
> ▷ Rise of temporary employment
> ▷ Employee leasing
> ▷ Wave of small business start-ups

■ Permanent downsizing

In the 1990s, downsizing became a common practice in companies and in the public sector. Most people have had a friend, relative, or neighbor who has lost a job since 1980.

But how is downsizing different from the layoffs people experienced in the workplace of the past? In the past, laid-off workers were often rehired when financial circumstances improved (in the 1970s, roughly half of laid-off workers were eventually rehired), but downsized jobs rarely come back. In the 1990s, fewer than 20 percent of downsized employees will ever be rehired by their former employees. As businesses restructure and reengineer to meet the challenges of the changing economy, they are eliminating millions of jobs forever.

■ Declining relative wages

Wages have become fundamentally unstable. Over the last decade, wages have declined steadily for the median worker. Median family income declined by 5 percent in the first five years of the 1990s. The average worker who loses a job today earns 15 percent less in his or her next job and many lose benefits like health insurance. In the last twenty years, the average income of families with heads of household under age thirty-four has declined by more than 20 percent (after adjustment for inflation). Workers' overall compensation has also been adversely affected as employers have shifted pension and health insurance costs to employees. Monthly consumer debt service (credit card interest) takes up 17 percent of the disposable income of the average person – a reality most young people know about all too well.

■ Underutilization of skilled labor

Over the next ten years, one out of every three individuals

graduating from college will go on to positions that don't require a college degree, almost twice the percentage of graduates who faced the same problem in the 1980s. The economy will create jobs for thousands of new cashiers, retail salespeople, waiters and waitresses, and janitors. Today, more than half of the jobs in each of those fields are occupied by workers under the age of 33.

Rise of temporary employment

The fastest growing industry in the West is temporary employment agencies. Today more than 90 percent of businesses use temporary staff. Manpower Inc., a temporary employment agency, is now the single largest employer in the United States, dwarfing other companies like IBM and General Motors. Altogether, more than two million Americans were employed as temporary workers in 1996, a 300 percent increase over the last ten years, and an employment trend that is picking up, not slowing down. These figures do not account for the hundreds of thousands of additional workers employed on a contract basis, as consultants, as part-time workers in second jobs, or those providing services through smaller companies on an outsourcing basis. Temporary employment is not just limited to office support staff anymore – now lawyers, engineers, medical technicians, computer analysts, paralegals, and even high level corporate executives are being marketed as temps. Soon, there will not be a staffing need that cannot be met through temporary staffing services.

Employee leasing

Employee leasing is *not* another term for temporary employment and the professional employment organizations (PEOs) that lease out employees are *not* just new forms of temp agencies. Employee leasing allows employers to utilize the work of their current and future employees without technically being their employer. The PEO becomes the employer, technically, and then leases out the employee to the organization where the employee actually works. If you are a leased employee, you still show up to the same place for work and work for the same manager and do the same tasks. But your personnel records will be kept by the PEO which is your actual employer and the PEO will pay your salary and benefits and has authority to hire and fire you. By leasing employees, instead of hiring them directly, organizations can free themselves from many human resources and personnel functions and also benefit from economies of scale on items such as health insurance, unemployment pay, and workers' compensation. One important consequence of leasing is that if you get downsized from one company, the PEO that actually employs you can move you over to fill an opening in one of the other firms to which it leases workers. And you can't even complain that you got fired because you didn't get fired, just transferred. After all, the company where you work never employed you in the first place. In 1997, two and a half million workers in the United States are leased on a 'permanent-employment' basis to the companies where they work. By 2007, that number is expected to rise to 37 million.

Wave of small business start-ups

There is a new wave of small business entrepreneurship. In the United States, for example, more than 54 percent of people aged 18–34 say they want to start their own business, nearly 10 percent aged 25–34 are actively working to start a business, and nearly 80 percent of the seven million US adults trying to start a business today are under age 34. In 1996, more than 150,000 new small businesses started up and created new work to be done for almost one million Americans. In fact, in the first half of the 1990s, small businesses (those with fewer than 20 employees) created work for seven million Americans net, compared with large companies (those with five thousand or more employees), which eliminated more than three million jobs net.

Is your head spinning yet? Clearly, the old-fashioned 'job' is in terminal condition. So what does the dying job look like now? For that, we look at the seven most powerful forces of change shaping the post-jobs era we are now entering:

> ▷ Reengineering
> ▷ Restructuring
> ▷ Technology
> ▷ Knowledge work
> ▷ Diversity
> ▷ Globalization
> ▷ The virtual workplace

Reengineering

Companies today are redesigning everything about the way work gets done. They are dissolving old-fashioned departments and bringing people and resources together along product and service lines or in ad hoc teams to address immediate needs. Work systems, which in some cases have been in place for decades, are being dismantled and refashioned to improve flexibility, efficiency, and effectiveness.

Restructuring

As industry reinvents its work processes, organizations are leveling out their hierarchies. Multiple layers of management are being eliminated and making way for fluid cross-trained teams which tackle whatever work needs to be done. There is no room for dead wood, at any level. While many workers are eliminated, those who remain as part of smaller core groups of permanent employees have more work to do than ever before, and these core employees must be prepared to perform a wide range of tasks from one day to the next.

■ Technology

Because of advances in technology, traditional boundaries are blurring – roles and tasks which used to be quite separate seem to be overlapping. It's no longer clear who is supposed to do what. It makes no sense for the boss to have a secretary type a letter, when the boss has a computer sitting right on her desk. It makes no sense to have a secretary do the filing when most files are stored in a local area network and can be retrieved with the press of a button. Offices still need support workers, but the support tasks that remain in the computerized office often do not occupy an entire day's work. That means support workers don't get full-time jobs anymore, unless they are able to carve out bigger roles for themselves.

■ Knowledge work

Most work today is knowledge driven – including clerical work, factory work, and retail service work. For example, secretaries no longer type, they use word processors; they don't file, they use database software. Workers in manufacturing don't operate welding guns anymore, they operate keyboards, which operate robots, which weld the steel on the assembly line. Today, you cannot work behind the counter at McDonald's unless you can operate a computerized ordering keyboard. That means no matter where you work, no matter what you are doing, you have to continually upgrade your skills. And, employers in virtually all fields are focusing more and more resources on training employees.

■ Diversity

While business has made important strides toward workplace diversity over the past several decades, employers increasingly must accommodate the changing face of the workforce: women, people of color, people with alternative sexual preferences, people with disabilities, people of all ages, and others right across the demographic map. The wide range of life experiences, perspectives, preferences, values, and styles of this diverse workforce is radically rewriting even the most basic expectations about ways of doing business.

Globalization

Multinational corporations have been pushing for globalization for decades. Advances in communications and transportation technologies have removed one barrier after another to international trade. With the dramatic geopolitical changes in the 1990s – the opening of Eastern Europe, the passage of the North American Free Trade Agreement (NAFTA), the General Agreement on Tariff and Trade (GATT), and the consolidation of the European Economic Community, to name a few big ones – few barriers remain. The doors are blown off the hinges: almost anyone today can buy from foreign suppliers, manufacturers, wholesalers, and retailers; sell to foreign companies and foreign consumers; tap into existing markets, open new markets, start up foreign ventures, take over and reinvigorate existing business entities.

Virtual workplace

The traditional boundaries of the workplace and the workday are fast dissolving. You don't have to go to a building to go to work anymore. With computers and modems, more and more people can work almost anywhere and anytime, as long as they have a place to plug in. With global time differences to accommodate and round-the-clock service to provide, fewer and fewer people can work from nine to five anymore. Many people today are already working from computer terminals and laptops in home offices, airports, hotel rooms, executive suites rented out by their companies nowhere near the company headquarters, or in hoteling arrangements. Offices in company headquarters are shared by several people because no one is there long enough to justify having his or her own office. People are more alone than ever at work, but also more connected than ever: The experience of working at a computer from a remote location is very solitary and atomized, but at the same time workers today are linked up to an endless network of people and information through the Internet, company computer mail, and voice mail systems.

What does this mean for careers?

Already, it is hard to find people working in old-fashioned jobs with clear parameters – job descriptions matching the work they do every day, regular tasks, fixed responsibilities, and uniform hours. Employers today require flexible workers prepared to do whatever needs to be done – that means continually upgrading skills, adapting to new conditions, assuming tasks and responsibilities in uncharted territory, working with one team today and another tomorrow, working eighty hours this week and twenty-five the next.

Relationships between employers and employees are no longer based on mutual loyalty, i.e. dues paying for job security. All work relationships are based on short-term mutual investments of added value: workers contribute their skills, knowledge, time, energy and creativity to create tangible results meeting the immediate needs of an organization, its customers, or its clients. In return, employers offer workers financial compensation, training and development, work experience, a chance to prove our abilities, and opportunities to build valuable relationships with people who may be able to help us in the future. These short-term mutual investments of added value are the basis of a new implicit workplace bargain between employers and employees.

■ What does this mean for you and me?

Even if we get hired by one of the global giants, or a small company, or a midsize company, we are exactly where we started: *on our own*. No matter how hard we work to get that perfect job, no matter how loyal we are to the company or the boss, our job is only as secure as the tangible value we can add today, tomorrow, and maybe next week. No one, absolutely no one, should expect to build a career around a long-term relationship with one employer. The nature of work and career has changed forever.

We have to become sole proprietors of our own skills and abilities, regardless of whether we work in what looks like an old-fashioned 'job,' or whether we are temps, consultants, or launching our own small businesses. No matter where we go, no matter what we do, we are in business for ourselves. We will need to take charge of our own lives and careers, look for self-building dividends in each new experience, adapt to constantly changing circumstances, stay flexible, and keep building from within.

■ Who will be our role models?

One of the biggest challenges of starting a career today is that the post-jobs era is brand-new for everyone of all ages. Those in their forties, fifties, and sixties, to whom we would normally turn as role models, are scratching their heads and trying to figure out how to navigate their own careers toward retirement.

If we cannot find realistic role models from among our elders, maybe we can find some among our peers. I haven't found a lot of young people out there who are doing every single thing right, but a lot of young people today *are* trying a lot of different strategies and they are finding out what works and what doesn't. From speaking with so many people of our generation about the strategies they are trying and the

A job was just a pile of shit anyway

If you believe *Webster's New Universal Unabridged Dictionary*, the *American Heritage Dictionary*, the *Oxford English Dictionary*, and a little speculation – the term *job* (six hundred years ago in the Celtic language – *gob*) originally referred to 'a pile of shit.' In the Middle Ages, there were a lot of piles of shit to clean up – that was a lot of the work that needed doing. Anyway, it's a long story, which I will spare you, but it actually makes sense if you think about it. Over the course of several hundred years, the word *gob* evolved: Eventually, *gob* was used to refer not just to a pile of shit, but to any pile. Later, the word came to denote a pile of tasks. Finally, *gob* became *job* and has been used for the last 150 years or so to refer to that pile of tasks that you do over and over again every single day at work. In other words, the meaning has come full circle.

different paths they are pursuing, I can say this much for sure: Success looks a lot different to those of our generation than it looked to those of prior generations.

As Generation Xers reinvent success, we are abandoning outdated assumptions, reinterpreting new trends, and instead of being discouraged, we are taking advantage of the radical shifts in today's workplace and learning to work in our own new ways. If you learn to work this way, you will invent your own great career in the workplace of the future.

Welcome to the post-jobs era

Chapter 2

In case you thought the end of the old-fashioned job was bad news, allow me to refocus the lens: welcome to the post-jobs era, where change equals opportunity.

The radical changes in today's economy are leveling the playing field for our entire generation. Experience and seniority are no longer king and queen of the job market. In the post-jobs era, it's your ability to add value that makes all the difference. As long as you can add value, your career does not have to be held back by the seemingly negative trends in today's economy. Not unless, that is, you are inextricably attached to the idea of getting an old-fashioned job.

Think about it: as much as you might be alarmed by the lack of an obvious career path, isn't there at least a part of you which has always dreaded the idea of getting a job? Who wants to get up at the same time every morning, put on a suit, go to the same office, answer to the same people, and take responsibility for the same tasks, for the same eight hours, every single day? Think of all those times people have asked you, 'Are you ever going to get a job?' Now, there is an easy answer: 'No. Never.' What a relief.

■ The new definition of a 'job'

While none of us will ever have a 'job,' in the old-fashioned sense, there is still a lot of work to be done. Indeed, every aspect of work is going through a fundamental transformation: what kinds of work we do, who we work for, when we do our work, how we do our work, and why we work. 'Jobs' are just not a great way to make a living anymore.

⌘ **Strategy:** *Stop thinking about getting and keeping a good job. Make a list of everything you can do that someone might want to pay you for. Sell your most valuable talents on the open market. Start working on one small project after another until you are working on several different projects for several different employers at the same time.*

❝ Nobody has a regular job anymore. Everyone is always looking around for the next project, either where they already work, or somewhere else, or both.

Public relations consultant, formerly a customer service staff person in an insurance company, twenty-seven

■ When you feel underemployed

The reason why so many highly educated, extremely capable people in our generation are stuck in service sector positions (in retail stores and restaurants) is simple: these positions are so readily available. Most of us can find two or three McJobs, if we try. Sometimes that becomes necessary just to pay the bills. If you have any breathing room at all, try to turn your situation to its best advantage.

⌘ **Strategy:** *First, if you are working in retail or in McJobs that you feel are not letting you maximize your abilities, then start maximizing the opportunity to become an expert at customer service. Customer service is one of the most valued skills in any workplace and you can practice that skill in any retail environment. Second, you immediately need to take on an additional project or job that you feel is worthy of you. Treat the worthy project seriously, as if it's your own business and work hard to develop it. Go back and forth trying to apply what you learn in each experience to each other experience.*

❝ I was working at an eye doctor's office as a receptionist and doctor's assistant. . . . I sold glasses, did contact lens training, dealing with files, calling insurance companies, answering the phone, dealing with the monetary trans-actions, I had to translate from Spanish to English because it was in a Latin community. . . . Then I also had to clean the office. . . . Everything I learned, he taught me, he gave me notebooks, tapes, and he would test me on it . . . so I had to study, which was a pain on top of the other studying I had to do at school. . . . But, it made me more independent, responsible, professional. . . . I think that's

> why I got the award for . . . best customer service . . . at
> my other job [working in a clothing store].
>
> *College senior, juggling several part-time jobs and internships,*
> *twenty-two*

▪ Make the most of temping

If you find that the best work you can get is temping, remember that temping is a fast-growing phenomenon because employers are desperately trying to adjust to an economy where staffing needs are erratic and unpredictable. Tasks come up over night that must be done immediately, even though such tasks may only need doing only once. The rapid growth of temping is a giant trend marker: long-term employment relationships don't meet the needs of organizations in a climate of rapid change and uncertainty. More and more, work is being arranged around immediate needs in short-term project-oriented employment relationships. Learn from the trend: prepare yourself to move from one short-term project to another, addressing immediate needs and adding value wherever you go. Soon, it will be as strange for a worker to have one employer as it would be today for a lawyer to have one client or a doctor to have one patient or a convenience store to have one customer.

⌘ **Strategy:** *If you find yourself going from one temp job to another, start using the experience to:*

- *Practice quickly adapting to new corporate cultures, new people, new tasks, and responsibilities.*

- *Use the experience to scout out further opportunities – not just a potential longer-term 'job' in the organization where you are temping – but, maybe, there are short-term projects underway to which you could add.*

- *Maybe you can see a need which is not being addressed and develop a proposal for how you would address it.*

- *Maybe you will build relationships with people who can help you.*

- *Maybe you can start racking up achievements which will help you prove your ability to add value in the future.*

❝ I started out thinking it was just a way to make some money while I figured out what to do with my life. . . . Then, I realized I was actually learning a lot. . . . In this one placement, I was actually there longer than a few of the so-called permanent employees. . . . When they offered me a job, I said, 'no' because I felt like I had a little more I wanted to get out of the temping thing. . . . I actually wanted to check out a few more companies.

Temp, twenty-three

■ The starting-your-own-business option

Maybe you've considered starting your own business. It's easier now than ever before because the three traditional obstacles to starting a business have all but disappeared.

1. *Capital:* When most new business start-ups were in the manufacturing sector, it cost a small fortune to capitalize a business. Today, however, most start-ups revolve around a service, often an information service, and any production that needs to be done can be done be a subcontractor and ordered just in time to meet the needs of a paying customer or client.

2. *The learning curve:* It used to make a lot of sense to go work for a while in an established company in the field where you wanted to start a business so you could learn the way they did things, get credentials, and then try to do the same thing better. But today new business thrives on innovation, on brand-new ways of doing things, and with the pace of change and technological advance, current ways of doing business become obsolete overnight. What matters most is how fast you can develop new ways of doing business to create services and products better and faster.

3.   *Job Security:* It used to be that if you went into business for yourself, you were risking something very valuable by giving up job security. . . . Yeah, well, not anymore.

⌘   **Strategy:** *Consider starting your own business. One way to experiment with being in business for yourself, without doing too much too fast, is through multi-level marketing (MLM) – otherwise known as network marketing. Here is how it works. Say Company X manufactures make-up. You become a sales representative for Company X. You sell their stuff and you get a cut. But you can also recruit other people to be part of your sales force and you get a piece of whatever they sell too. And, the people you recruit can recruit others and everybody gets a cut . . . and so on. If you are interested in MLM, pick up a magazine like* Worth *or* Success *or* Entrepreneur *– they usually have at least one article or some ads in the back about MLM opportunities. If you are one of those people who is suspicious of MLM because it sounds like a pyramid scheme, that's cool. There are plenty of other ways to experiment with starting your own business.*

❝ [Wherever there is] a need for someone with my skills . . . [the ability to] implement some financial accounting software, and do the whole thing from start to finish, at a low rate, and make it cost effective, I would be able to do that project . . . and if I could get a bunch of projects to work on, I guess I might be creating my own consulting business.

Computer systems consultant, worked for big six accounting/consulting firm, lived a year in Budapest, worked for a mid-sized consulting firm, now working part time and applying to graduate programs, twenty-nine

▪ Make flexibility your mantra

Don't worry. McJobs, temping, and starting your own business are not your only options in the post-jobs era. While they're not offering old-fashioned 'jobs' anymore, lots of old-established organizations, fresh from reengineering and restructuring, are still ready to hire plenty of young, talented people. In fact, it matters a whole lot less than ever to corporate decision makers how long you have been in the workforce, where you have worked in the past, or how long you worked there. There are fewer people in charge and there's a lot more work to be done. Those in charge don't care very much about levels of authority anymore. They care about results. That means you can compete with anyone of any age for the best assignments, as long as you have the skills and knowledge to get the job done, to address an immediate need, to fill an important gap in the team. The only thing that really matters is what you can do and what results you can achieve.

You can still work for years in the reengineered, restructured organization, but you won't be climbing a ladder. Most of the moves you can make are lateral. You can stay in the same organization as long as you are prepared to keep moving laterally, regularly reinventing yourself and your role.

⌘   **Strategy:** *Be flexible and ready to adapt your role within the organization to meet new demands and address emerging needs. Identify and keep a running list of new tasks you are capable of doing; responsibilities you are prepared to assume; new and improved ways of solving old problems – and new ones.*

❝ I've worked for the same company for five years and I have had, like, fifteen different jobs since I've been here. I am always the one to suggest a new project I'd like to take on. When the company announced this big reengineering initiative, a lot of people were freaked out. For me, it was just another chance to reinvent myself.
Constantly reinventing himself in a large financial services company, twenty-seven

Reinvent the definition of 'support staff'

If you find yourself in a lowly support staff position, answering phones and doing photocopies, don't lose heart. Technology is eliminating many of the distinctions which used to separate primary tasks from support tasks. Support functions are probably not the only responsibilities you have. Chances are, whomever you are working for will give you as much responsibility as you can handle. They may not call it a promotion and they may not give you a raise – be cool with that for now. Decision makers are looking for reliable people they can depend on. Teach them to depend on you whenever something really important needs doing. Regardless of your title, your job will be defined by whatever you are actually doing. You are the only person with the power to transform your job and give yourself a 'promotion.'

⌘ **Strategy:** *If you are working in a position that is traditionally a 'support' role, identify important tasks and responsibilities, seize them, and be the person decision makers want to depend on. Give yourself a promotion first – then go ask for a raise.*

> “I don't care what you call me. Nobody gets through to my boss without talking to me first. Yeah, I get her a cup of coffee if she asks for it, but she also does her own letters. Well, I do the envelopes, but that doesn't bother me. . . . And, in the last three months, I have written two speeches for her and two articles for publication under her name. . . . Okay, I'm a secretary. Whatever. Give me a raise.
>
> *Secretary to policy adviser in a busy political office, formerly worked as a temp, also worked as a research assistant, attending graduate courses in public administration, twenty-eight*

Initiate a plan for continuous learning

If you feel like your formal education has not fully prepared you for the real world of work, you are not alone. Even if you manage to get a job in the field you studied in school, you will still need continuous training. Things change so fast in today's world; everyone needs continuous training. That's why there are more company-sponsored training opportunities available today than ever before, no matter how unskilled or short-term your actual job may be.

Even if you are flipping burgers at a fast food restaurant (the ultimate McJob), don't forget that McDonald's, Burger King, and Wendy's are major international corporations with more training resources than many prestigious institutions of higher education. You may be able to get your manager to sign you up for company-sponsored training in subjects like customer service, sales, quality control, computers, and inventory systems. Maybe you can get yourself onto the manager's training program. Of course, no matter where you work, it will be easier to get your employer to commit substantial resources to your training if your tasks and responsibilities are more challenging and require more instruction. That means you may have to take on some challenging work to earn your way into some of the better training opportunities.

⌘ **Strategy:** *First, do every bit of the training that is required for you to do the tasks you were hired to do. Then, go after more. Be on the lookout for all official training courses and materials, and sign up, whether they are intended for employees at your level, or not. Also, look out for external training programs, seminars, and university courses where you can learn transferable skills and see if your employer will pay for you to attend.*

> “I figured, if I am going to work at McDonald's, I am not going to just stand around here all day making minimum wage. I got my manager to let me do the assistant manager's training. I was assistant manager for a while and then I went right into the manager's training too, but I was out of there pretty fast. It was just the point of it. I was like, as long as I am here, I am going to do whatever they offer. And a lot of that was just general retail management. It made a big difference between my

experience there and the other people who were working there. I actually walked away with something pretty valuable.

> *Small business owner, formerly worked throughout high school as bus boy, also worked behind the counter at McDonald's, and as assistant manager, thirty-one*

■ Leverage your uniqueness

If you've always wondered where you fit in, not quite fitting in with the crowd may turn out to be your special niche. Is there something which sets you apart from the mainstream? Maybe you are part of an ethnic minority, or you grew up in a rare geographical location, or you are gay, or you speak a foreign language, or you have a physical disability. In the workplace of the future, diversity can be a valuable competitive advantage. Those who bring diversity to the workplace will be valued more and more as they help organizations better understand, connect with, and maximize increasingly diverse markets. Not only that, but in a marketplace where organizations must innovate in order to compete, those of diverse backgrounds will be valued for their different perspectives because a new perspective often gives way to redesign, revision, and renewal.

⌘ **Strategy:** *Identify something in your background or experience which sets you apart from the crowd and qualifies you to help an organization better understand, connect with, or maximize a particular market. Or, think about ways to leverage your unique perspective to drive innovation.*

❝ Maybe my being gay made some people uncomfortable in that job, especially at first. . . . But, it was so obvious they were overlooking a niche market in the gay community. I suggested they start targeting special travel plans for couples in the gay community. . . . There were niche publications that it made sense to advertise in and, where you could use pictures that might freak out readers in other publications. . . . There were a lot of dimensions to it. And it wasn't like, you know, I was the gay guy handling the gay market. . . . It was just that I understood a market they hadn't tapped into.

Planner of incentive meetings, formerly worked as messenger,
also as freelance writer, twenty-six

❝ You know what, the fact that I speak Spanish makes me more valuable here. I don't care what anyone says, I get paid more money because I can talk to more customers. I think that is only fair.

Credit card information line operator, formerly
worked as telemarketer, twenty-four

■ Globalize yourself

Have you ever thought about packing it in, packing it up, and taking off on a long trip around the world? Doing just that might be one of the best career moves you could possibly make. With the globalization of markets, any real knowledge of foreign countries – geography, culture, people, language – is a critical and unique asset, for which many organizations are willing to pay serious money.

If you have traveled extensively, lived in another country, studied a foreign culture, or mastered a foreign language, you have probably acquired experience and knowledge that is very marketable. You could sell yourself as a key player in any international transaction: translate incoming and outgoing correspondence; participate in conference calls as an interpreter and to help explain cultural idiosyncrasies; travel abroad with senior execs as a translator and meeting facilitator or just go along as a tour guide; help foreign entrepreneurs trying to open up foreign markets; work as a diplomat; become an importer/exporter.

⌘ **Strategy:** *Travel abroad, learn a language, a culture, and a foreign city, and then come back home and sell your global knowledge.*

❝ When I started studying Nepali, I wasn't thinking about

the future career benefits this would have. After being in India and Nepal for 14 months, I invested my last $1000 in jewelry, clothes, etc. and descended on the apartment of my good friends in New York. Then I schlepped out to the streets and sold, sold, sold. I made enough to go back to Nepal and stayed there for another 15 months. I came back to the US a second time, again with merchandise to sell, and began to think a little more seriously about the future. At that stage, I could have parlayed my knowledge into being an importer/exporter. When I went back to Nepal for the third trip, I brought the addresses of graduate schools with me and sent off for applications. A year later I found myself enrolling at Cornell, and I am working toward my Ph.D. in anthropology now – the career that I'd chosen, without realizing it, several years before.

Anthropology graduate student, traveler, former flea market merchant, worked for a while right after college in a computer company, thirty

■ Become a virtual worker extraordinaire

Maybe the thing you feared most about facing adulthood and getting a job was having to show up at the same place every day at the same time and conform to a nine-to-five schedule. Forget the nine-to-five drudgery. In the post-jobs era, the workday never ends: If you always have your laptop with you, when do you get home from work? If your home is your office, when is it too late to call? If your most important client wants you to call her at 9.00 a.m. in Germany (when it's the middle of the night in America), what time does your day begin? If both you and your spouse or partner have demanding work lives, how do you balance work with your relationship, your home life, your children, and recreation? In today's climate of intense competition, the lack of boundaries in the virtual workplace can make it harder than ever to keep the demands of work in their proper place – or easier than ever.

⌘ **Strategy:** *Take advantage of telecommuting, flexible*

schedules, and virtual office technology to fulfill extremely demanding work responsibilities however and whenever they fit into your life. You'll end up doing more work, under more convenient circumstances, and you'll have more time to devote to your family and personal life.

> ❝ I can see why a restaurant manager wouldn't want me working from 1.00 a.m. to 5.00 a.m. because there wouldn't be anyone there to serve. But if I am working on an audit report in the middle of the night and then feeding my daughter at 5.00 a.m. so my wife can sleep. . . . If I do the rest of my work all day Saturday and Sunday. . . . If that is what works best for my family, why should the client care? Why should the partner care? Who cares when an audit report is written as long as it's a really good report?
>
> *Audit staffer at a big six accounting/consulting firm, twenty-six*

I hope I have succeeded in getting you to rethink the radical changes in today's economy and in getting you excited about working in the post-jobs era. Please – let go of outdated assumptions. Look at the obvious trends in today's economy and get ready to pounce on them. Learn from those of our generation who are inventing a whole bunch of new ways to work. Try some out and invent some new ways of your own. Take charge of your career, stay flexible, and keep building yourself.

Voracious learning

Chapter 3

❝ I want to work in an environment where I can just keep learning new things every day as much as possible, which is why I am currently thinking of leaving where I am now.
Electrical engineer, twenty-five

❝ Pretty much every decision I have made in my career to date has been about putting myself in the line of fire of new skills.
Sales representative for consumer products company, started in the company as a clerical temp, twenty-six

❝ I don't care if I am watching TV or reading a magazine or driving through town or working out or talking with my friends or whatever, all I'm doing is soaking up information. My goal in life is to be a sponge.
Juggling part-time jobs as radio DJ, personal trainer, and bartender, twenty-eight

❝ What has made college so incredible for me was not any one class or any one professor or any one book or anything like that. I made a decision early on that I was going to pick one thing each semester that I was really going to master – really focus on that one thing and over time, I built up this arsenal of things that I know really well, and they are all things that I really wanted to know about. And, it is like my own personal collage of knowledge and skills.
College senior, twenty-two

❝ I want to do research and take on mental challenges. I would say, 'Give me more intellectually demanding work.' It was a little bit competitive – my boss and I were always competing to get the mental challenges. When I went to work for this Korean foundation, I was writing speeches, running seminars, and everyone was so enthusiastic. It was really exhilarating. My writing improved because I was writing a lot and getting a lot of practice. Now, I am thinking of going to graduate school.
Temp, formerly worked as research assistant and then as office manager for a public interest organization, also worked as a program officer for a foundation, twenty-seven

66 I think people here think I am kind of a pain in the ass. I
think people I worked with at my last job did too. But I just
won't leave it alone unless they take the time to explain
things to me. Like, one time I got it in my head that I was
going to learn how to use this new software and anybody
who knew anything about it – I just wouldn't leave them
alone.

> *Working in new market development team for large manu-*
> *facturing company, formerly a manufacturer's representative for*
> *the same company, worked in big six accounting/consulting firm*
> *for a while right after college, twenty-eight*

66 The only way I learn is by doing. So, I may do a shitty job
the first time, but the second time it will be better. And the
third or fourth time, I know it. That's how I learn.

> *Administrative assistant, twenty-three*

Why is voracious learning so important?

What characterizes our generation, perhaps more than any
other trait, is our voracious appetite for information. This
appetite leads many people in their forties, fifties, and sixties
to think that Xers have short attention spans: to them, it
seems, we ask too many questions and expect instantaneous
responses; demand more information than we can possibly
sort through; seek constant feedback from the world around
us; interrupt a lot; and always try to change the subject in the
middle of a conversation. What do they expect? Of course we
think and learn differently from our elders. After all, we are
children of the information revolution. Our minds were
shaped by a tidal wave of words, sounds, and images coming
at us from all directions all the time. Well, thank goodness for
that, because our rapid-fire style of thinking and learning is
going to be critical to our survival and success in the
workplace of the future.

Already, continuous learning is absolutely necessary just to
survive in almost any workplace. The number one challenge

we all face is keeping track of the endless amount of information being produced every day, from an infinite number of sources, on every conceivable subject (and plenty of inconceivable subjects). How do we decide where to focus? There are so many choices to be made: What subject? What facts, techniques, perspectives are we going to master? In what medium do we feel like learning today? What sources should we use? How do we choose among all the images and sounds and text out there?

The key is multiple focus. Picture this: you are sitting on the couch with a snack resting on one knee, your homework on the other knee, the remote control in one hand, and the telephone in the other hand (creating a market for call waiting). As you can see, multiple focus should come rather naturally to people of our generation. Being able to juggle a lot of different images, sounds, and texts coming at you from different sides all at once is a valuable skill (not evidence that we have short attention spans).

Many of the same people who think Xers have short attention spans are tuning out the tidal wave of information because it makes no sense to them – the images seem random, the sounds are noise, the texts speak nonsense – especially if it pours out all at once. Those who tune out are destined to be clueless, but those who can tune in will have a huge advantage: we have a better chance of making innovative connections among seemingly unrelated strands of information. Those innovative connections generate new knowledge, which is a prime commodity in today's information-driven economy.

> ❝ I can't count the number of times I have been working on a problem and people keep saying to me, 'This thing has nothing to do with that other thing,' and I am just thinking to myself, 'Not yet, not yet.' But of course, when you see connections among things that other people don't see, that's how you invent something new.
>
> *Research scientist, twenty-nine*

If you use multiple focus to juggle a lot of different strands of information, you will also need to master selective elimination. Keep asking yourself, 'Is this going to be on the test?' (Another no-brainer for those of our generation.) The thing is, it's your life and career, so you get to decide what's on the test. To be an effective learner in today's information environment you must have the ability to make strategic decisions quickly about what you are going to learn and, more important, what you are not going to learn. Then shut out all the distractions and concentrate on the specific information you've decided to master. This is not lazy – it's absolutely necessary.

> 66 You've got to explore, definitely. But, you've also got to stop and concentrate once you latch onto something pretty concrete. Otherwise, you have a lot of interesting thoughts and ideas, but they never crystalize into what I would consider knowledge. If I just tried to read the sports news every day alone, it wouldn't be easy to keep up with, and I would be on a par with half the world.
> *Sports journalist, formerly worked as assistant to the publisher of a now defunct national sports publication, twenty-nine*

Everywhere you look, the pace of change is accelerating rapidly. One day we are going to the ATM machine. The next day we are swiping our ATM cards at the grocery store and asking for cash back. Soon, we will go shopping in on-line grocery stores. If you happen to be an expert on ATM machines, your knowledge may be obsolete in five years. With rapid change comes a steep obsolescence curve: ways of life become obsolete. Ways of doing business become obsolete. So do knowledge and skills. And the truth is, much of what you will need to know in five years hasn't even been discovered or invented yet. That's why it's so important, in today's world, to be a voracious learner.

■ Create your own opportunities to learn

If you feel you don't have sufficient opportunities to learn wherever you are, you may have to create your own. You can easily design your own customized learning opportunities in each of the following spheres:

  ▷ College
  ▷ Paraprofessional apprenticeship (such as being a paralegal)
  ▷ Graduate school
  ▷ Corporate world

College

If you don't get a college degree, you put yourself at a tremendous disadvantage in the marketplace. If you do get a college degree, you may saddle yourself with a huge financial debt before you are even out in the world getting a running start. And what do you have to show for it? If you graduate with a specialized degree in a career-oriented major, such as teaching or social work or computer programming or physical therapy, you may have a hard time marketing yourself outside that field. At the same time, you may have just as hard a time marketing yourself inside that field until you somehow work around the infamous Catch-22: you can't get a job without experience and you can't get experience without a job. Here's the flip side of the higher education dilemma: four years of liberal arts study may make you a lot smarter, but it's very hard to market yourself on that basis alone. No wonder so many leaders in higher education are wondering out loud how colleges and universities are going to stay relevant in coming years.

So what?

If you are a student, you need to figure out what you love to learn and then take more responsibility for getting the education you want and need out of college. Know the score up front about the real world that awaits you. Use college to build the knowledge, relationships, experiences, and behaviors which will help you survive and succeed. Customize your college experience and maximize the tremendous resources available from one of these incredibly underutilized learning machines.

Take control of your own college experience

1. Design your own major (such as computer modeling to predict future sports team performance based on player statistics) or shape your own unique curriculum (political campaign strategy on the Internet) within an established major (political science).

2. Redesign your classes so that you can emphasize the aspects which interest you the most – study your favorite parts disproportionately and choose your papers, projects, and presentations to focus on what you want to learn.

3. Treat the hard parts of any class (the parts you cannot avoid) like push-ups or sit-ups – use them to exercise your brain and make it stronger.

4. Design your own self-study course – come up with books to read, papers to write, a research assignment – and go sell a lecturer on taking responsibility for supervising you and ensuring you get proper course credit.

5. In any class: use homework to practice time management; use tests to practice performing under pressure; use research assignments to explore subjects that interest you; use papers to practice your written communication skills; use class discussion to listen carefully and practice making brief, precise comments; use class presentations to practice speaking in front of a group.

6. Turn your lecturers and tutors into mentors by expressing thoughtful interest in the subjects that mean the most to them, in which you also share.

7. Create learning circles with your friends. (Learning circles are groups of people with common interests who get together to learn with and from each other.)

8.   Recognize and make the most of all the resources that are uniquely available to students, such as first-rate libraries, free on-line services, student discounts on virtually everything, the other people on campus (students, faculty, and staff), free lectures on campus, concerts, exhibits, performances, and the ability to call virtually anywhere in the world and get them to talk with you and provide tons of information just by saying, 'I am a student and I am writing a paper . . . '.

9.   Turn college life into a learning lab: use the student loan process to learn about credit and financial management; use organizations, clubs, sports and other activities to practice interpersonal skills, teamwork, and leadership; use life in a hall of residence to learn how to live in close quarters with other people; use partying to learn how to work a crowd or, maybe, to get a little crazy.

10. Seek part-time jobs during school, summer jobs, and placements which will expose you to real world situations and give you an up-close preview of some of the fields you may be interested in. While there, learn new skills, meet people who can help you in the future, and complete tangible products which you can point to later as proof of your ability to add value.

11. If you need to do McJobs during school or summers to make enough money to survive, remember that there are 168 hours in every week – you have time to balance two jobs: one for money, one for growth. But don't discount all of the hidden learning opportunities in any job, no matter how menial, repetitive or difficult.

> 66 As an undergraduate, I designed my own interdisciplinary program. To begin with, I was a double major in environmental studies and geography, and this allowed me to learn about both the physical world and people's relationships to it. I chose my classes very carefully. Participating in an environmental group, I gained skills working with people and learning about the environmental arena. After college, I did the park ranger thing because it was fun, and

it was a chance to experience nature first hand and care for the thing I was going to be working for. . . . I have sought out workshops and conferences. Most of the reading I do is learning about the natural world. I chose the graduate program I'm in now because it gives me the flexibility to link different disciplines instead of being stuck in traditional thoughts and traditional career paths. It allows me to mix hard science with social science, which is the way I think the real world works. There is no one else doing what I am doing in terms of my emphasis, my angle, the mix of courses I am going to take. I have the advantage of knowing what I want to do and what I need for that specific field, which is also a relatively new field.

Full-time graduate student in forestry, after spending two years balancing part-time jobs, placements, and part-time graduate study, twenty-four

■ Paraprofessional apprenticeship

Tap into this trend: the amount of work available for paraprofessionals ('almost' professionals) is increasing dramatically in all of the traditional professions such as medicine, law, engineering, architecture, accounting, and academia. Paraprofessional work, in fact, is one of the fastest growing forms of work in the economy. Why?

1.   The cost of having services performed by doctors, lawyers, engineers, architects, accountants, and Ph.D.s (for a few examples) is astronomical compared with the cost of having those services performed by nurse practitioners, legal assistants, technicians, draftspeople, tax preparers, and graduate student teachers.

2.   In the post-information revolution world, it is harder and harder for professionals to maintain their traditional monopolies in their specialized fields of knowledge. There is so much information available that laypeople can buy do-it-yourself books and magazines, look stuff up on the Internet, watch documentary television, and

so on. The boundaries between professional and para-professional work are breaking down.

3. With so many professionals typing their own letters, checking their own voice mail and pulling up their own files on a local area network (instead of some file room), those in support roles have the time to handle more substantive work.

4. It is in the interest of all parties for paraprofessionals to assume more and more traditionally 'professional' responsibilities.

So what?

While there are many functions still which must by law be performed by legally licensed professionals, there are also many which need not be. If you place yourself in a support role in a professional environment, you can accumulate as much professional-level responsibility as you are able to accomplish. With a less expensive and less extensive course of training (often nothing more than on-the-job, sink-or-swim training), you can become a *de facto* medical technician, legal assistant, bookkeeper, architectural draftsperson, engineering technician, or whatever. The more you are able to do, the better it is for you and for the professional who is employing you. You learn skills, build valuable relationships, achieve results that help you prove your value, and try out a profession without committing to a full course of graduate study. The professional who employs you gets a lot of very important work done at a fraction of the potential cost. And you might decide to invest in becoming a fully accredited professional yourself.

Ideas for turning your paraprofessional job into an apprenticeship

1. Ask your boss for funding and time allowances to pursue every formal training opportunity, including night school, live seminars, home study books, videos,

audiotapes, CD Interactive, and on-line services. If you are willing to take on very important work at a fraction of the potential cost, you'll get the funding and time to get more training.

2.   Attach yourself to one or two professionals and treat them as professional learning mentors – ask a lot of questions.

3.   Seek assignments in new skill areas, but always leave a lot of extra time, ask for clear guidelines, a model to copy, and a professional to remain available for questions and quality check.

4.   If it's legal, do it – try to get as close to the boundary of professional practice as you can, without the proper credentials.

5.   Once you master an important task, take full responsibility for it so the professional comes to depend upon you for it.

6.   Learn one or more skills of the profession, which you may be able to market in your own consulting business later on.

" At a medical walk-in clinic, I was hired as a receptionist. The position actually encompassed things like spinning blood, assisting the doctor with minor procedures, calling in prescriptions to the pharmacy, taking and recording temperatures. Lunchtime consisted of a series of two-minute periods when I would run to the back room and scarf down as much of my sandwich as I possibly could during the rare occasions when we were caught up with the patients' charts and as long as the doctor was in with a patient. I returned every Christmas vacation, all summer, Thanksgiving and spring break because I could work so intermittently, because she simply needed me too badly – and I learned so much.
Administrative director in small consulting firm, used to work
part-time in a medical walk-in clinic, also worked as a temp,
twenty-three

■ Graduate or professional school

Let us look at four common paths for graduate study in, for instance, the United States.

▷ *Law:* There are almost a million lawyers in America, and 40,000 people get JDs each year, after three years in law school, and then spend two months studying for the bar exam (which feels like another three years, trust me). After all of that, it's pretty hard for new lawyers to get a good job. Between 1985 and 1995, there was a 15 percent increase in the number of law graduates who could not find work as attorneys.

▷ *Academia:* The 40,000 new Ph.D.s who enter the academic job market each year, after six to ten years of graduate study, find themselves competing for a very small number of jobs. Often, there are hundreds of qualified applicants for each new position. As a result, many of the most highly educated people in the United States today are forced to work outside their field while applying year after year after year for jobs that don't exist.

▷ *Business:* Applications to MBA programs are increasing again (by 7.5 percent in 1995) and almost 200,000 people will apply to MBA programs this year. The best among the 50,000 who complete the two-year MBA program this year will go right down the water slide into high-pressure corporate jobs, working eighty hours a week or more, until they get rich or burn out. Many others will find that their degree is too general and not prestigious enough to get them the kind of job they were hoping to get.

▷ *Medicine:* Every year, 25,000 new physicians enter the American pool of physicians after completing four-year MD programs (about a third of these new doctors come from foreign medical schools). After a grueling postgraduate training, which lasts several years, these new doctors enter a healthcare industry dominated today by managed care organizations, insurance companies, bottom- line-oriented hospitals, bureaucrats, politicians, and other non-physician decision makers who constrain the ability of today's doctors to practice medicine.

So what?

Getting a graduate degree is extremely time-consuming (it takes years) and it can be very expensive (it can add tens of thousands or more to your debt). The sad truth is, a graduate degree is not necessarily a ticket to a successful, gratifying career. So, be careful. Take it from a guy who went to law school and then practiced law for 428 days. Don't do it!

Yes, there are many transferable skills you can pick up in most graduate programs, but there has got to be a better way to pick up those skills without spending years of your life and putting yourself deep in debt. I often think of what I could have done with the five years and $80,000 dollars that was invested in my 428-day legal career. Yes, it's a credential, but paper credentials mean less and less in the post-jobs era. The question will always be, 'What can you do?' And remember, graduate training is the most specialized training there is, so it's going to answer the 'What can you do?' question pretty definitively. If you are going to go to graduate school, make sure you want to do the work you are being trained to do.

How to take control of your graduate school experience

1. Don't get a graduate degree just to get a credential – a piece of paper is not necessarily 'something to fall back on.'

2. Make certain that a graduate degree is required to do the work you want to do.

3. Investigate alternative paths of training and credentials (such as apprenticeships).

4. Explore all financial aid options, grants, scholarships,

fellowships, sponsored placements, and related work opportunities to lighten the financial burden.

5. Use your time to build one or more specialties within your field – accumulate special knowledge and skills that will help you establish your own niche in the field.

6. As an up-and-coming professional, cultivate professional relationships with your peers, faculty, visiting speakers, academics at other schools, practitioners in the field, professional associations, potential employers and all the other high-level people to whom you have special access while in graduate or professional school.

7. Start racking up professional accomplishments – speak at conferences, do experiments, studies, projects, papers; write, publish, teach, invent; do your thing and prove yourself, at no risk.

8. If there is a good career placement service in your graduate school, use the recruiting water slide to, at least, get wet and test out the waters of the profession. There will be no easier process for getting fast-tracked into the neighborhood of some good positions in your field (even though they may not last more than a year).

> 66 From undergraduate professional school (engineering), I took a job with a medium-sized company that designed, produced, and marketed high-tech communications products. The next move was to pursue higher education at night while still working full-time. I was able to learn new skills and, best of all, the company paid for most of it. It enabled me specifically to land an interesting assignment and not be pigeonholed into the technology where I already had developed an 'expertise.' Then, I realized the path open to me in the current job I was in was not where I wanted to be. So the logical, easy choice (all too easy): go back to school, and particularly a program that will yield a well paying job so that you can repay all those loans. Law school it was, which was a wonderful haven from working life where I was able to recapture that education experience. After law school, I

took a job at a large law firm. [I was] funnelled in that direction. [After less than a year there], I had the opportunity to clerk for a judge and I decided to take advantage of it [because] it would be interesting and also would give me a varied experience and stand me apart from those with just law firm experience.

Working as law clerk for a judge, formerly an associate at a large law firm, used to be an engineer, thirty

■ Corporate world

Corporations today are turning themselves into 'learning organizations,' in which facilitating the continuous education of their employees is a core business function. The learning organization is made necessary by four main factors:

▷ There is so much information produced on any given subject in any given week that time and resources must be allocated just to keep up with the flow of information.

▷ Because new developments emerge so rapidly, basic knowledge and skills become obsolete continuously and must be replaced routinely with up-to-date knowledge and new skills.

▷ Training technologies have advanced so much in the last decade that cutting-edge companies are turning training excellence into a serious competitive advantage, setting high standards for the competition and forcing the rest of the corporate world to chase the trend. While training and development budgets used to be considered a luxury in much of the corporate world, today, smart companies are investing heavily in their internal education resources.

▷ In order to attract and retain the smartest and most capable workers, companies have to offer good training programs and plentiful learning resources.

So what?

Training resources are precious and training is a costly investment. What good is it to Company X if they spend a lot of time, energy, and money training us and then we leave and go use that training working for another company, maybe even a competitor? This is why organizations are trying more and more to concentrate their training resources on employees who will stick around for a while. Managers must try to predict what kind of return they are likely to get from investing training resources in one employee as opposed to another. Thus, a new class system is emerging in organizations today: the to-be-trained class and the not-to-be-trained-more-than-necessary class. Those most likely to become semipermanent (two to five years) core group employees will be the first priorities for formal training, while the shortest-term workers will be excluded from most formal training opportunities. Of course, there is also a growing premium on workers trained at someone else's expense – so the would-be core-group employees will be in high demand with plenty of offers to job-hop.

How to maximize formal training opportunities

1. Get yourself high up on the priority list for training and get some important decision makers committed to your training needs.

2. Volunteer to serve on the training committee if there is one (or form a committee if there isn't one).

3. Make it your business to know the corporate training schedule by heart and become a walking training calendar.

4. Always sign up for every training program (whether you are eligible or not).

5. Whether or not you are eligible for a particular training program, try to get yourself advance copies of the training materials – worksheets, handouts, books, audio and video tapes – and start learning the material on your own.

6.   When you do attend trainings held at conference centers, don't waste them staying up all night drinking beer. Maximize the opportunity: stay tuned in during class, read the materials and complete the worksheets, ask questions, monopolize the trainer's time, and be the person everyone is coming up to afterwards to ask questions.

7.   Seek projects at work – before, during and after any trainings – which will augment and reinforce the training.

8.   Come up with ideas for new knowledge or skills to be included in the training curriculum, then research your idea and develop it into a detailed proposal (who, what, where, why, when, how) for the training program you hope to see included.

9.   Find an outside training opportunity (courses at the local university, seminars, books, home-study videotapes, whatever). Then write a one page answer to the question 'Why would this training make me a more valuable employee?' Present this page to the decision maker whom you ask to authorize payment for your outside training. Maybe you can even find outside courses you can audit for free.

10.   Don't limit your vision of appropriate training to material necessary to do your current tasks and responsibilities. Instead, expand your vision to include anything else you want to learn about or can benefit from learning about.

> **❝** They have incredible training resources but it has to be very much self-initiated. If you don't do anything, the training would be a lot less. You have to be very aggressive to get more information about what training is coming up. At the beginning there is quite a bit of guidance, like they say, 'Read this stuff,' and then they point you in the direction of the courses you are supposed to take. But after that, if you want access to the best materials and

courses or the best teachers or get training in a particular area of expertise, you have to go and make the effort to do that. They spend so much money on training, it would be really stupid not to make the most of it. But remember, they don't hold your hand.

Consultant in a large management consulting firm, twenty-five

■ Don't let obstacles stand in the way of your learning

In your drive to learn voraciously, you are certain to run across plenty of obstacles. Maybe you can't find an established program in the field you'd like to study. Or you are not eligible for the kinds of programs you can find. Or you don't have time. Or you live too far away. Or you can't afford it. Believe me: what you can afford least of all is to let those problems hold you back. Most problems can be solved if you put your mind to them.

? **Problem 1:** You cannot find a graduate or college program because you are not eligible or you can't afford it and you've been turned down for the scholarships, loans or work-study grants which would help you fill the financial gap.

Solution: create your own schooling

1. Set concrete learning goals and design your own curriculum (decide what you want to learn and make a plan for all the subjects you want to cover and all the materials you will need).

2. Go to a university library (or community college or search on-line) and study course descriptions in the course catalogues to get ideas for what kind of curriculum you might want to set up for yourself.

3. If you see courses in the catalogue that you would really

like to take, go to the academic department within the school which offers the course and ask the department secretary for a copy of the course syllabus, so you can get some ideas for organizing your own self-study class.

4. Whatever you decide on for courses, you will have to take some time to plan. Can you do more than one class at a time? What information will you cover each week? What materials (books, articles, movies, experiments) will you use?

5. For each course, find at least one person who knows a lot (or at least something) about the subject at hand (a friend, co-worker, family member, shopkeeper) and appoint her/him as your professor (you don't even have to tell the person). Make a point to discuss the subject with this person as often as you can.

6. Try to find real-life opportunities to apply what you are learning.

7. Keep a journal with questions which come up and record the answers as you are able to uncover them. Don't be discouraged if the list of questions with answers is short and the questions without answers is longer.

Another solution: create an apprenticeship program for yourself

1. Find a mentor who is successful in the field you want to learn about.

2. Design your model apprenticeship and write a proposal specifying what you would like to do, how you would do it, what role you want your mentor to play, and don't forget to specify the parts you are unsure about.

3. Offer yourself as unpaid labor for several months, in exchange for the mentor's commitment to teach you (you won't be making any money, but there won't be any

tuition either and maybe you can get a place to stay for free or at least an occasional meal).

4. Work as hard as you can with no expectations at first, but keep your eyes and ears open, and try to develop informed expectations.

5. Keep a journal of every single new thing you learn.

6. Keep a journal of the new things that you really want to learn and go over the list once a week with your mentor, trying to plan some time to meet your learning goals.

? **Problem 2:** There is plenty of formal training where you work, but you job-hop a lot. The result: you are neither in one place long enough to get trained nor are you in the to-be-trained class because your employers don't expect you to stay very long.

Solution: turn job-hopping into a customized training program

1. Use the first stage in the job search process to gather information and find out more about the jobs, organizations, and industries that are out there.

2. Use your initial letters and phone calls to develop your communications skills – learn to write brief, penetrating letters and speak with a calm, confident and persuasive voice.

3. Practice your interpersonal skills during interviews – master the art of making a good first impression and the art of evaluating a person quickly.

4. Use interviews to practice extemporaneous speaking – use every hook to bring yourself back to a smooth, well-rehearsed story of how you have added value in the past and how you will add value in the position at hand.

5. Use each interview to practice building a quick rapport with a perfect stranger.

6. Learn the best business practices by comparing (silently) work methods from one organization to the next . . . and the next . . . and the next.

7. Learn about corporate culture from comparing organizations.

8. Try to add at least one new concrete skill to your repertoire during your orientation period in each new organization – maximize each opportunity for the new organization to teach you some basics and let you work your way up to speed for a while.

9. Pick out mentors in each new organization and build relationships with your mentors that will last much longer than your relationship with any organization.

? **Problem 3:** There is no formal training program where you work.

Solution: design your own training program

1. Get someone else in the organization committed to your learning goals – they will be your allies (secretaries, flunkies, senior managers, peers, clients, suppliers) and you will support each other's efforts to learn.

2. Aggressively seek out learning resources (books, professional publications, files, software, on-line resources, finished products which you can copy) and study them.

3. Be a copycat: find someone who knows how to do what you want to learn and watch carefully.

4. As soon as you master one task or responsibility, ask for a lateral movement to a new task or responsibility – if possible, in a new skill area.

5. If the organization can't move you laterally often enough, request a task or responsibility in a new skill area which you can learn by doing at your own pace,

while balancing the other tasks and responsibilities which you already know how to do.

6. Demand FAST feedback – *f*requent, *a*ccurate, *s*pecific, and *t*imely – so you can constantly find out exactly how to keep doing the things you are doing right and change the things you are doing wrong.

7. Use the office setting to learn office skills: telephone persona, letter writing, faxing, filing, interacting with peers and superiors, and looking busy.

? **Problem 4:** The flow of information where you work is all clogged up. People are not talking. Memos are not circulating. You're not in the loop because there really isn't one.

Solution: force a square peg into a round hole

1. Tell anyone who tells you 'You don't need to know': 'Yes I do!'

2. If you are having a hard time getting questions answered, circulate the questions on paper or e-mail to everyone in the organization and solicit answers from anyone who cares to respond. If you are not getting answers, think of more and more creative ways to pose your inquiries and keep trying until someone answers.

3. Find some of the more informed people and if they won't talk to you, try talking to their assistants or secretaries for information.

5. Study files from past projects similar to the one you want to learn about.

6. Call from the outside and pretend to be a customer or client and find someone who will answer your questions.

? **Problem 5:** You are working in a McJob and feel that
the training opportunities are not up to your needs and
abilities.

Solution: turn your McJob into a customized training program

1.   Learn to master human relations by dealing with your
     co-workers, bosses, and customers.

2.   Learn the art of customer service by serving your
     customers.

3.   Master the art of sales by selling.

4.   Become an expert on inventory by paying attention to
     ordering, delivery, stocking, and restocking cycles.

5.   Learn about marketing by paying attention to the
     marketing efforts of the organization (they probably pay
     top whack to the top professionals for that stuff).

6.   Conduct your own market research by asking customers
     a lot of questions.

7.   Conduct your own frontline quality research by keeping
     a journal of which products and services you think are
     great, good, fair, not so good, and terrible. And try to
     think of ways to improve the products and services at
     every level.

8.   Learn to manage by being managed. Watch your
     manager and learn how to recruit, select, train, schedule,
     and reward employees, as well as how to resolve
     conflicts and handle emergencies.

Finally, no matter where you are, no matter what you are
doing, turn your every day life into a learning lab:

▷   You are surrounded by information resources – people,
     organizations, companies, the government, libraries,
     books, magazines, newspapers, television, radio, the
     Internet. Use them.

▷ Don't be afraid to ask stupid questions if you are totally in the dark about something. If you have to, ask one dumb question after another until you refine your inquiry enough to start asking good questions.

▷ Learn the art of the blind phone call – call anyone in the world without identifying yourself and ask lots of questions. Call the library, the newsroom at a newspaper or radio station or television station, an organization, a company, or a government agency, an expert in the field, or whomever you want. If the first person you call doesn't answer your questions, call back until you find someone who will. If one person gets sick of you, call someone else.

▷ Use shopping to learn about inventory, customer service, retail display, retail management, and negotiation skills.

▷ Use driving or walking or riding a bike to learn the lay of the land.

▷ Use arguing to practice the art of persuasion.

▷ Volunteer for political campaigns to learn about politics; for any charity to learn about fundraising; for the homeless shelter to learn about the homeless; try out for a play to learn about acting; tell jokes at an open-microphone night to learn about stand-up comedy; or sing at a karaoke bar to learn about singing; or box at the gym to learn about fighting.

▷ Do all of the above also to learn basic work skills, gain experience and perspective about the world, pick up mentors, and practice being an effective value adder.

▷ Get your family or friends to teach you about the stuff they know about.

▷ Learn to cook by cooking; to clean by cleaning; to garden by gardening; to golf by golfing; and so on.

Voracious learning is a philosophy and a way of life. It's about believing that every square inch of the world holds an infinite number of lessons and that every single moment of your life is an opportunity to soak up as many of those lessons as you can. Keep your mind open, your eyes looking, your ears hearing, your nose smelling, your taste buds tasting, and your skin feeling – no matter where you are or what you are doing. The world is full of information: be a sponge and soak it up.

Learn what you love

Chapter 4

So, you want to be a sponge? If you are going to dedicate yourself to voracious learning, you'll have to decide what to learn. Many people will tell you that the most important rule for learning in today's world is this: 'Make sure that what you learn is marketable.' Here is an important corollary to that rule: *anything you learn is marketable.*

Say you know about saxophone players in Asia. Kind of obscure? Perhaps, but think about how you can leverage this knowledge as a commodity: maybe you could write an article for a magazine that focuses on Asia or on saxophones or on music in general or on politics (what are the foreign policy implications, considering President Clinton plays the saxophone too?). You could create a proposal for a saxophone company about how to exploit the Asian market more fully. What about other wind instrument companies? Maybe, if the sax is catching on in Asia, there is room for the clarinet or the tuba. What about organizing a trip for American saxophonists to visit their counterparts abroad? Or, vice versa, bring the Asian saxophonists to America as part of a cultural exchange.

Let me say it one more time: anything you learn is marketable. So, above all else, learn what you love to learn, whatever that may be. That is the real secret to becoming a voracious learner (if you are not already). If you focus on learning what you love, then learning will be a pleasure – you won't be able to get enough.

> 66 My sister has severe arthritis and growing up with a sister with disabilities has affected me and made me want to work to help people with disabilities. I became very interested in barrier free design, which is designing someone's home environment in a way that allows them to become more independent, like adjusting the counters in a kitchen so that someone in a wheelchair can use it. I wanted to do something that had something to do with architecture and I wanted to do something that had to do with disabilities. I started to do some design work and through the university I did an internship at the

Smithsonian in Washington and I worked on some exhibits and got to use a computer aided design program (CADD) for that. I got the internship at the Smithsonian because I had excelled in the AutoCad computer aided design class. I took the class more seriously than a lot of other people and that semester I spent a lot of time in the lab practicing it. Where other people found it tedious, I found it stimulating. I took it more seriously because it was a key competency in doing design on the computer and a skill I could use to differentiate myself so I wanted to master it. The real thing was that I could see the uses I would make of it in the future for doing barrier free design.

Parlayed placements into a position at a public interest organization dedicated to special housing needs, twenty-four

▨ What do you love to learn?

If you are not sure what you love to learn, it's easy to figure it out. Make a point of catching yourself in the act of learning. What magazine articles or book passages do you find yourself stopping at and reading intently? Do you ever find yourself going back over a sentence, a paragraph, a page, or a chapter? When you are flipping around on TV or surfing the Web, what kinds of shows and Web pages capture your attention? What were (or are) your favorite classes in school? In the classes that you didn't like or were only lukewarm to, was there anything that really captured your attention for a little while, like a particular book or a particular class discussion or a particular project? What kinds of things do you like to talk about? What do you like to do in your free time? What kinds of things do you find yourself doing over and over again because you really want to get it right? What kinds of things do you find yourself spouting out facts about, that you picked up somewhere and remembered for some reason?

Keep a journal for a couple of weeks and make note of every time you catch yourself learning. After a couple of weeks, look back and see what subjects or skills have most captured your attention. Politics? Sports? Statistics? Food? Sex? Health? History? Literature? Entertainment? Education? Electronics? Animals? People? Environmental issues? Nature? Writing? Speaking? Hunting? Doing experiments? Hiking? Building or fixing machines? Fishing? Massage? When you identify the combination of subjects and skills that appear most in your journal, then you've found what you love to learn, and that's where you need to focus your learning energy.

▪ Turn what you love into transferable skills

While you are voraciously learning whatever you love to learn, you need to master as many key transferable skills as you possibly can. Transferable skills are skills which can be applied in almost any job in almost any workplace. It's worth making a point of learning what you love in ways that help make you more valuable no matter where you work, no matter what you do:

> ▷ Focus on results (the ability to set clear goals and meet deadlines).
> ▷ Adapt to new situations and circumstances quickly.
> ▷ Manage information.
> ▷ Think critically.
> ▷ Define and solve problems.
> ▷ Communicate well (verbally and in writing) and relate to people.
> ▷ Become a great team player.
> ▷ Negotiate and resolve conflicts.
> ▷ Master foreign languages and foreign cultures.
> ▷ Gain technological competence (mostly computers and the Internet).
> ▷ Do what matters most to you.

I call this list of eleven skills 'the core curriculum for the post-jobs era' and it covers 99.9 percent of what people mean when they talk about transferable work skills. As you build your own unique repertoire of all the things you know and all the things you know how to do, remember to work on building these transferable skills in yourself. Look for opportunities to practice them in everything you do – in school, at work, and in your daily life.

■ Focus on results

Setting clear goals means being able to answer the question 'What should I have in my hands when I am done?' If you are a salesperson, your short-term goals might be:

1.   Build a list with twenty prospective customers.

2.   Make twenty phone calls.

3.   Speak to at least five live bodies (leave messages for the rest).

4.   Send follow-up letters to the five people I speak to.

5.   Get at least one to agree to meet with me in person.

But what good are those goals if you don't hold yourself to deadlines?

Strict deadlines are how you keep yourself on track – if you have to have something done by Wednesday, work long hours Monday and Tuesday, so you are not frantic when the deadline comes. And strict deadlines help you measure your effectiveness – if you are not meeting your deadlines, you will have to reassess your goals (maybe they are not carved up into small enough chunks) and how you work (maybe you are getting caught up in too many time wasters).

⌘   **Strategy:** *It helps a lot to carve up goals into bite-size chunks, such as results that take thirty minutes or an hour to achieve. Over time, you will find that breaking big projects into bite-size results will make you more effective.*

> ❝ I don't care what it is, if we are in a meeting or my boss is getting all excited about something, I just want to know, 'What do you want me to do? And when do you want me to do it by?' Don't worry, if I have questions, you'll hear from me.
>
> *Assistant account executive at an advertising firm, twenty-four*

■ Adapt to new situations and circumstances quickly

People who are too attached to the way things are have a hard time learning new skills, performing new tasks, doing old tasks in new ways, working with new machines, new managers, new co-workers, new customers, new rules, no rules. Usually, the greatest difficulty for such people is the uncertainty – not knowing what will be (or not) just around the corner.

Don't be one of these people. Learn to love change.

Master today's changes and tomorrow's uncertainty because things are going to keep changing, with or without you. That means when you realize that the organization you work inside is in a permanent state of reengineering just to keep up with the pace of change, don't freak out. Be one of the few people who is willing to do whatever is needed, whenever it's needed, whether it is something you already know how to do or not, whether it is supposed to be 'your job' or not, whether it is something you love to do or something you are going to have to just tolerate for a few weeks or months.

Be flexible enough to go, on any given day, from one boss to another; from one team to another; from one organization to another; from one set of tasks to another. At any given time, you may be balancing three part-time 'jobs' or moving from one short-term project to another or working a day job and starting your own business or doing all of those things and going to school at the same time. To move seamlessly between and among these different spheres every day, you need to be as adaptable as a chameleon.

⌘   **Strategy:** *If you are temping, use the experience of going from one company to the next to practice adapting yourself to new workplace environments. Or you can practice adapting by volunteering for a bunch of different organizations over the course of a year (an AIDS organization, a political party, a pressure group).*

❝ I have had jobs since I was fifteen. I started telemarketing newspapers. Worked at Taco Bell. Then at this telephone survey place. In college, I have had two or three jobs at once. I was working in the financial aid office. I worked in an eye doctor's office. I worked in two clothing stores, in one as a sales rep and the other as a cashier. I worked as an operator at Ernst & Young, answering phones and sending out faxes. I worked at First USA Bank as an operator. And, right now, I have two internships, one at a radio station and one at a television station. Like, I am twenty-two and I've seen a lot. There is nothing that is going to surprise me, I'll tell you that much. I have learned to be pretty flexible.

College senior, balancing multiple part-time jobs and placements, twenty-two

■ Manage information

There is so much information to manage these days, it is a good thing we have sophisticated technology at our disposal to conduct research and to organize, analyze, and store valuable information. But technology won't manage information all by itself, and neither information nor technology can be maximized without people who are shrewd about framing research inquiries, accessing resources, gathering the right data, understanding, interpreting, and thinking of interesting ways to use the data. In an information driven economy, those skills are critical.

⌘ **Strategy:** *Choose a project in your work or school or home life that requires you to manage a lot of information. For example, the family finances, or a research paper, or a presentation you are working on for a client. Choose a project that will give you a chance to practice new and better ways of managing information. Experiment with a new filing system. Break in a new database program. Check out a new search engine on the Internet. Be very conscious of how you are framing questions when you do research, how you are going about identifying sources, and how you are gathering and interpreting data.*

❝ One of the reasons I am staying in school part-time right now is that I have access to such a great library and free access to the Internet. I think one of the reasons I got the job I have now is that I really played that up – I can do on-line research for free. I am in the library a lot. And I think it has affected the kind of work I get, too. I am always trying to find ways to fit work and school together, which means I am always coming up with papers to write that don't have much to do with the class, or suggesting projects to my boss that come right out of an assignment.

Research assistant in a public advocacy organization, taking graduate courses at night, twenty-four

◼ Think critically

Critical thinking does not mean criticizing, disparaging, or finding fault. It means differentiating between reliable and unreliable information, carefully weighing the strengths of conflicting views, and making reasoned judgements. Critical thinkers do not leap to conclusions – they take the time to consider various possibilities and do not become too attached to one point of view. They do not latch on to one solution – they know that most solutions are temporary and improve over time with new data. Critical thinkers are, at once, open to the views of others and supremely independent in their own judgements.

⌘ **Strategy:** *Try to catch yourself jumping to conclusions. Think of a few things that you take pretty much for granted. Can you prove it to yourself? Now, stop and question your assumptions. Consider the other side. See if you can make an effective case for the other side. Also, try making a list of all the things you just don't know about the matter. At first, practice this critical thinking drill in private. You don't want to sound like you're up to your ears in self-doubt, especially since critical thinking skills should fill you with self-confidence. All knowledge is provisional, but the ability to figure things out is definitely a keeper.*

❝ When I was interviewing for jobs right out of college, I got a bunch of call back interviews to go to visit different companies and interview with a bunch of people at each one. As I would go from one person to the next in a company, I started noticing slight disparities in things like how flexible are the hours or is there an open-door policy or how much room is there to move around to different parts of the company. Everyone had a different story. And I was trying to figure out the real story. So I started pressing a little harder and a little harder and some people would practically spill their guts, like I touched on a nerve. Once the evidence was all in, I was able to figure out the real story on my own.

Consultant in a management consulting firm, recently finished MBA, formerly worked as analyst in investment bank, twenty-six

▪ Define (and redefine) and solve problems

The key to defining a problem can be found in one word: *because.* 'This doesn't work' states a problem but doesn't define it. 'This doesn't work because it's not turned on,' defines the problem. Turning it on is the easy part. Of course, sometimes solving a problem is just as hard as defining it: 'AIDS is deadly because it destroys the immune system.' Okay. Well, even though we have defined the problem, coming up with a cure is going to take a lot of time and effort.

But don't stop there. If one definition of a problem doesn't yield an immediate solution, it's time to look for a way to redefine the problem: 'People contract AIDS because they engage in unprotected sex.' Okay. This definition of the problem implies a solution – at least a provisional solution: Don't have unprotected sex. When you have trouble solving a problem, keep redefining the problem until a solution is implied by the definition – at least a provisional solution. The trick lies in your imagination (and your critical thinking skills).

✂ **Strategy:** *The next time you are faced with a seemingly intractable problem, try playing the game 'What's wrong with this picture?' Then, keep playing until you've defined the problem from many different angles – enough that you have a range of possible solutions. If you are having trouble looking at the problem from different angles, take a giant step back. Try asking yourself why this is a problem for someone in particular or for something in particular. 'This is a problem for_____' will imply very different solutions depending on what you put in the blank. For example: 'Global warming is a problem for people in New York because if the polar ice caps melt, New York will be flooded' implies one range of solutions (such as, people living in New York should move to higher ground) while 'global warming is a problem for people with fair skin because ultraviolet rays will get much stronger' implies a different range of solutions (such as, people with fair skin should cover up). You can play this game ad infinitum with any problem. It is one of the more subtle, but also one of the most important, problem solving strategies you can possibly learn.*

❝ If I'm facing a problem in a deal I'm working on, I may need to step back a day and do a little research. I may need to say to the partner I am working with that 'I am not going to be able to give this to you tonight, I am going to have to give it to you tomorrow.' Sometimes you need a little time to learn something new, to pick up some important substance, that helps you look at the problem from a new angle.

Lawyer, twenty-nine

■ Communicate well and relate to people

How do you get the thoughts and feelings that live in your head into someone else's head (when you want to)? If you can make yourself understood, you have a better chance of connecting with people, getting others to share your interests, influencing their thoughts, and even persuading them to do the things you might want them to do. However, there is an element of communication that is much more important than speaking and writing and being understood, namely listening and reading and understanding what others are thinking and feeling.

⌘   **Strategy:** *Practice careful listening: Don't interrupt when others are speaking and don't let your mind wander. First, ask open-ended clarifying questions, such as 'What do you mean?' or 'What would be an example of that?' or 'What else?' Then ask specific questions, such as 'Do you mean ____?' or 'Are you saying ____?' to make sure you understand. Try asking yourself (or the text) the same kinds of questions when you are reading.*

❝ Working at The Gap definitely gives you people skills. You have to really learn how to read people. You have to figure out what people want, whether people want you to be aggressive and help them or laidback and leave them alone. You learn how to determine their needs, how to approach people. Sometimes people know what they want and sometimes you have to ask them questions and help them figure out what they want. You have to learn to keep asking questions. I have developed certain interpersonal skills with people and come out of my shell. If I am really looking to find something out, I know how.

Graduate student in speech pathology, working part-time as graduate assistant for a professor and part-time at The Gap, has juggled several part-time jobs (mostly retail) since high school, twenty-three

◼ Become a great team player

Here is a tough balancing act: maintain your independence and be a great team player at the same time. You don't want to sacrifice your creative autonomy, but you can't have everything your own way. You don't want to give away your best ideas, but you want to make valuable contributions to the group. You want credit and recognition for your individual accomplishments, but you also want to share in the group's successes. It's nice to have company, but, sometimes, you'd rather be left alone. Often, it feels like it would be easier to do five times more work on your own than to deal with the needs, expectations, and idiosyncrasies of a group of team members. But you don't have that option. Most work these days is being done by short-term, project-oriented teams because most projects require more expertise than any one person can offer – each person on the team brings a necessary element of knowledge and experience to the project, and together the team can do things that no one person could possibly do. So learn to be a team player with the understanding that as soon as you get used to one team, it will probably be time to move on to another . . . and then another and another one after that.

⌘ **Strategy:** *Look for opportunities to practice being on a team: sports, politics, charity, fundraising, or at work. Decide up front that you are going to sacrifice some of your autonomy; you are going to contribute some of your best ideas and hardest work; give up some of the individual recognition you might receive and try to win recognition for the group. And, decide up front that you are going to learn*

*as much as you can from the other people on the team,
build relationships with some of the other team players, and
take pride in the group's success. For personal credit and
recognition, try to be the person that everyone else in the
group would nominate for 'best team player.'*

❝ We develop an incredible bond and become a real support
network for each other, which is good, because we are
also a source of stress for each other. I rely on all of these
people to leverage their experience, to give advice and
help, because these are people of all nationalities and all
backgrounds, and tapping into their knowledge helps me
do better work.

*Working on the internal audit staff in a global
industrial giant, thirty*

■ Negotiate and resolve conflicts

There are four keys to negotiating and resolving conflicts:

▷ Make sure you are talking to the person with the power to
make a decision (or at least influence the decision); otherwise you are wasting your time.

▷ Find the common ground: Is there anything that all (or
most) of the interested parties agree on? The common
ground is usually the reason why you are talking (I want
to work for you and you want to hire me). If we both want
some of the same things, we can both win. Win–win is
where we want to end up, so it's a good place to start.

▷ Identify each party's bottom line, especially your own. If
you know your own bottom line (you know you cannot
pay me more than £300 per week) it is much easier to sort
out what is possible and what is not (if I am asking for
£350, maybe we can make a deal; if I'm asking for £1000,
forget about it).

▷ Who has the 'walk-away power'? The more you have at
stake in the deal (working for you would be the biggest

opportunity of my life), the weaker your negotiating position (I would work for you for free if I had to). If you can walk away with minimal loss, you are in a very strong position.

But walk-away power is not enough, nor is identifying your bottom line or the other party's bottom line, nor is finding common ground, nor is talking to the decision maker (or decision influencer). To be effective, you need to wield all four of these elements simultaneously.

⌘ **Strategy:** *If you don't have a lot of opportunities to nego-tiate, practice by going into any retail establishment and trying to negotiate the price of a standard retail item. For one thing, the reactions of the salespeople are pretty funny because most people do not assume that retail items are negotiable. You may be surprised to find, however, that anything is negotiable, even prices in a retail store: Just say, 'Is that your best price?' Then you will probably get to speak to the manager and try the same thing: 'Is that your best price?' If they have any room to move, you'll get a lower price. Trust me – I've done it many times. Keep in mind, though, that if you keep getting thrown out of stores, you may be negotiating with a little too much fervor.*

❝ I worked in two different stores and people are very odd. They will return a shirt because they spilled coffee on it and the stain won't come out. I have to be very nice but explain why we can't let them return it because it is not a defect in our product and we can't resell it with a stain. Now, it's a different case if the zipper broke or there was a defect and then of course we are going to have to take it back. But, there are those cases in the middle, or where the customers become irate and then you have to bargain. And you have to make them feel like they have been successful. People will try to return things from two years ago and they may be worth nothing to the store, and the person may come in wanting a certain amount. So, we have a book we can check and show them what they paid

> for it and what the mark down in value is over time and showing them this number in the book helps them see that's all I can do. When I first started, if there was a problem like that, I would call up a manager . . . and I used to feel like customers were sort of attacking me. But, now I am very comfortable handling things like that myself.
>
> *Student, working part-time in retail, twenty-three*

Master foreign languages and foreign cultures

Start thinking 'international': With global markets opening up, you can set yourself apart from the crowd just by being multilingual. A command of major European languages would be a great asset for doing business in the European Union. Spanish opens up additional possibilities in South America (and think about the the large Spanish-speaking communities in the United States). If you speak Russian or Romanian or Ukrainian, you could be helping some of the entrepreneurs who are setting up businesses in brand-new Eastern European markets. And, as Tom Peters says, 'Think Asia': more than half of the world's 6.5 billion people live in Asia. That's a market worth tapping.

Imagine trying to do business with someone who doesn't speak your language – it would be pretty hard. That is why learning a foreign language is so valuable. Go one step further: learn a foreign culture, so you know what's appropriate and what's not (when in Rome, do as the Romans do). One step further still: learn your way around a foreign country, and then you will make a hell of a tour guide when you go back with your new boss (who wants to penetrate this foreign market) in tow – and while you're abroad, you'll be in charge because you will be the expert (your boss will be the one nobody can understand).

⌘ **Strategy:** *Read some travel books, pick a foreign country you'd like to visit, buy the appropriate book and keep it on* *your desk as incentive while you memorize vocabulary words and mimic language tapes until you are blue in the face. Meanwhile, save up as much money as you can. Then go live abroad for a while, but don't live among Westerners abroad or in hostels with other young tourists. Find a way to live among people who speak the language you want to learn and can show you around and from whom you can learn about the culture. Ideally, try to find a family to live with.*

If you can, try to get working papers and get a job while you are abroad. If you don't want to go abroad, just get the books and the language tapes and study your heart out. You'll find plenty of opportunities to use what you learn right here at home.

❝ I wanted to learn French, so I went to France. It seemed like a good place to learn the language. It was really weird and uncomfortable at first. I had taken French in school, but it was nothing that prepared me for living with people who didn't speak any English at all. I lived there for quite a while and I got a pretty good job with an investment bank, and when I came back home, I was working in the main office in New York. I was the only person there at my level without an MBA, practically, and it was great because I had great contacts in our Paris office. . . . And, you know, who do you think got to go along when my boss had to go to Paris?

Analyst in an investment bank, traveler, twenty-eight

■ Gain computer and Internet competence

I walked into a fast food restaurant a few weeks ago and there was an older woman behind the counter having a very hard time working the new computerized cash register (which is about the most user-friendly machine in the universe). She was getting very frustrated and I heard her say under her breath, 'I've been gone for five years and now I'm useless.'

When I talked with her a little bit, I learned that she had worked for this fast food restaurant for fifteen years until she left for five years with a disability. Now she was back and everything had changed. Everything was computerized – the cash register and the drive-up ordering system, the ovens and the french fries maker, everything. But this woman is not alone. There are many, many people – mostly older people – who are terrified of technology, especially computers (these are the same people whose VCRs perpetually blink 12:00). To them, the Internet sounds like science fiction. But pretty soon, it will be as weird to not be on-line as it would be to not have a telephone.

Of course, plenty of technophobes are high-powered decision makers in some of the biggest, most important organizations in the world – they just hate computers. Most, however, are smart enough to know that keeping up with cutting edge technology is necessary for any organization to remain competitive – technology makes work faster, more efficient, and more accurate. If you don't know how to use a word processor, a database, a spreadsheet, and the Internet, you had better learn how. Quick!

⌘   **Strategy:** *Every school and every organization has at least one staff person who is in charge of computers – he or she is usually the in-house 'expert.' Hang out in the computer center for a while every day, build a relationship with one of these techies and then start grabbing one for twenty minutes every day to ask questions. Get him or her to sit down with you and walk you through some basics of word processing, database use, or a spreadsheet program, and getting on-line and functioning on-line. (Maybe there is something you could teach your new techie friend in exchange.)*

Also, consider buying a couple of self-teaching books and maybe take a computer class. The very best way to learn the technology is to use it on a concrete project – if you don't have one, invent one to experiment with.

❝ When I got there, it was a small office, two very entrepreneurial people who had been friends for years. Neither of them knew how to use the computers. There were computers in the office, but neither of them knew how to use them. One still doesn't, the other does now because I taught her and she is very grateful. . . . They had three really old Macs and you would literally do a press release, put it on a floppy disc, come over to another computer, and say, 'I have to print something out' because the computers weren't hooked up. No one could ever find anything because all the documents were on floppy discs. It took some convincing, but I went out and bought some new computers and I networked them together myself, and it is huge now that we are networked. We generate a lot of work and they definitely know that. Right now I am trying to learn a lot more on the Internet. Everyone says it is the future of everything. We have a client now and I am trying to publicize their Web site on-line and use that as an excuse to learn more about the Web.

Working in a public relations firm, formerly an aide in a US Congressman's office, before that worked in customer service for American Express Platinum, also worked for a while as an 'event gypsy,' twenty-eight

❝ I've gotten great things from the Internet. I subscribe to two different discussion groups on my professional interests, and I've sent out a number of inquiries and gotten back an amazing amount of information that I'd never have had access to. I used it, for example, to create a list of people working in my particular specialty area. I asked people to to e-mail me with their contact information if they were interested, and then I provided lists for people in the group – which was not only useful for me personally, but actually made me a bit of a 'leader' in the growing new field. Just by doing this, I became a key person whom one would contact for information, and I've been in direct correspondence with over half the people on the list.

Historian, twenty-nine

■ Do what matters the most to you

What matters the most to you? Say it's your family. Then what happens when you have a conflict between working all weekend and attending your child's birthday party? No-brainer. Unless, of course, missing work this weekend would cause you to actually lose your job and cause you to no longer be able to support your family. Again, no-brainer. But what if you are not being honest with yourself? Maybe what's really at stake is that if you don't work this weekend, some of the people at work won't like you as much. Which is more important to you, being popular at work or being there for your children? Again, no-brainer.

Maybe you can figure out a way to do both: what if you could get up at 3.00 a.m., Saturday and Sunday, work like a dog, and then go to the birthday party too? You won't get any sleep. What is more important to you, getting sleep this weekend or meeting your obligations at work and being with the kid? Again, no-brainer. What if you could fake it, make it look like you were at work . . . or just stop by the kid's party, you know, make an appearance? What is more important to you, being genuine and really meeting your obligations or 'looking good' to others and getting away with doing less? Again, no-brainer. If your priorities are clear and you stay in touch with them, it makes a lot of seemingly tough decisions a whole lot easier.

⌘   **Strategy:** *The next time somebody asks you to do some-thing that you really don't want to do and you feel compelled to do it, ask yourself this question: 'Am I considering this because it is what really matters to me, even though it may be difficult or inconvenient or not fun or get in the way of other things I need to do – or is it because I want to be popular with this person?' Or, the next time you find yourself procrastinating about something that you really need to get done, ask yourself 'Are all the things I keep doing, instead of the thing I really need to do, more* *important? Do they matter more to me? Or are they just easier, more fun, or more convenient?'*

❝ No matter what, if I am on Mars, I am going to work out every day, for at least thirty minutes. It affects my mind and my energy and how I look and feel. I would quit my job if I had to, if it somehow got in the way of my well being.

College senior, twenty-one

❝ There have been times when my boss will tell me to call a client and lie. I am sorry, there is no way I am ever going to do that. If you want to be a sleaze, that is your problem. There is no way I am ever going to pick up the phone and tell a bald-face lie to a client . . . no way.

Lawyer, thirty-two

As you focus on learning the things you love to learn and master the core curriculum for the post-jobs era, you will be building your own unique repertoire of knowledge, skills, and wisdom. I promise that your repertoire of learning will be marketable. The key will be positioning yourself and your repertoire strategically in the marketplace of added value. That is what Chapter 7 is all about. Chapters 5 and 6 are about building relationships with people who can help you.

Beyond
networking

Chapter 5

❝ You have to take responsibility for relationships. If you don't invest the time in building relationships, you are going to be pretty lonely.

Teacher, twenty-eight

❝ Don't even try to do it alone. The other people in your life who love you and like you and care about you – your family, friends, coworkers, whoever you get close with – those people are going to carry you through the bad times.

Bookstore sales clerk and multilevel marketing entrepreneur, formerly fast food restaurant assistant manager, at one time on welfare, thirty-two

❝ Almost every job I've had has been because someone recommended me. You know, you don't get recommended by people who don't know you.

Six jobs in two years, twenty-four

❝ I spent a lot of time working with this one senior partner who seemed very powerful. If I had this guy on my side, I thought I would be in pretty good shape. I came back from a short vacation and he was gone. I mean for good. They voted him out. So where does that leave me?

Lawyer, twenty-seven

❝ Even if I am going to be here for just a while, I am going to meet someone who can help me. I try to collect people.

Temp, twenty-five

❝ Basically, she said, 'Why don't I become your mentor?' She has taught me a lot about how to deal with people. What to expect. And she is only a few years older than I am, but I have a lot of respect for her.

Working in a clothing store and juggling two placements, twenty-three

Relationships are the most reliable institutions in the post-jobs era

If your life fitted the stereotype of the world in which our parents grew up, you would graduate from college and get a good job in a good company in a nice community. You would get married and you and your spouse would buy a house (with a thirty-year mortgage) near a good school, and you would expect someday to pay off the mortgage and have a mortgage-burning party. By then, of course, you'd be ten years from retirement, so you wouldn't be going anywhere until you earned that gold watch.

Imagine living forty years in the same community. You'd know lots of people: The people who attend your church or synagogue or mosque; the people who belong to community groups; the same old crowd who always volunteer for fund-raising events; the people on the school board or the Parent Teacher Association; your neighbors; your co-workers.

In the old days, when so many people stayed in the same community for most of their lives, it felt like relationships pretty much took care of themselves. But our generation grew up in the wake of the baby boomers' disruption of so many social norms and the discrediting of the grand institutions which traditionally have anchored communities (families, neighborhoods, schools, government, business, charities). As baby boomers turned away from institutions, our generation lived in the chaotic aftermath of their choices. Many people our age spent a tremendous amount of time alone as children – either because our parents both had to work, or our parents did not stay married, or they were permissive (in keeping with the in-vogue parenting style of the seventies).

> 66 When my parents split up my mum took us one night at midnight on a plane and went back to Connecticut from Seattle. That made me grow up a whole lot faster. I remember all the different apartments we lived in. Since graduating from school, I've moved around a lot – lived in

Seattle, traveled for a while, lived in Washington, now I live in New York. Next who knows?'

Former 'event gypsy' (traveling as a flunky for the Goodwill Games, the NCAA tournament, and other events), also worked as an aide to a US Congressman, currently working in a public relations firm, twenty-eight

❝ I remember being scared a lot of the time when I was a kid, for no good reason. I was just alone a lot of the time and the world seemed really scary. So I learned to be very independent. But I also learned to really value the people that I could make friends with.

College senior, twenty-two

❝ When the house I grew up in was leveled, paved over, and turned into a pizza place, I knew that I could never really go home again.

Film maker, ice skating teacher, used to work as a paralegal, also teaching a college film course, thirty-one

Mass unemployment devastated communities that had relied on traditional heavy industry. Many families split up or moved or both. New bypasses, lined with retail outlets, skirted around towns and cities. And new housing developments popped up everywhere to pack in the new suburban diaspora. This was not a return to neighborhoods and a renewal of community, but, rather, the next stage in the atomization of society. Everybody was inside, completely isolated from one and other but also strangely connected to the same cultural messages via television. As established institutions ceased to be the center of life (pushed along by the 'Me' generation), individuals turned inward.

Self-reliance became the mantra of the day and independence has replaced the old community ideal. And then the corporate world jumped on the self-reliance bandwagon – leaving individuals to fend for ourselves in an environment of fierce competition.

❝ The company I work for is going into this reengineering. It's like, 'Okay, prove yourself from now on.' Thanks, that's great. A lot of us have tried to pull together, to help each other get through the changes. But, it's going to last a long time.

More jobs than he could count, all in the same
financial services company, twenty-seven

The irony of the new culture of self-reliance is that individuals need each other now more than ever. We live in such a rapidly changing world there is very little firm ground in which to drop anchor. So we need to anchor each other.

Since we can no longer depend on the old-fashioned con- nections, based on common affiliations with established institutions, we need to focus on building long-term relationships with individuals. Cherish your family and friends. And, remember, in today's world, people are in constant motion. So as you pass through institutions, latch on to mentors, students, co-workers, managers, subordinates, customers, clients, vendors, and suppliers – and stay in touch because neither you nor they are likely to stay long in the institution where you find them. You will have to maintain these relationships yourself, in constant motion, with no anchors.

■ Invest in long-term relationships with individuals

Those individuals with whom you connect and maintain contact over time will be a critical source of support and security. Together, those individuals will become the most reliable institution in your life – perhaps the only reliable institution.

■ Location doesn't matter anymore

With the rapid advancement of communications tech- nologies, location is no longer the determining factor in maintaining relationships. It doesn't matter where you are. As long as I have your contact information, I am going to stay in touch with you. More and more, our permanent contact information will have little or nothing to do with our location. I'll reach you in cyberspace. Or, contact you on your permanent personal phone number attached to your 'personal communicator' (which I recently saw advertised in a telecommunications products catalogue). Soon, those personal communicators will be able to send and receive not just voice and text but video images as well. Already cars are turning into mobile communications centers. You could be on the other side of the world and we could still pal around via the Internet.

> 66 I was working on a long-term project with a team of five people. It was near impossible to find times that we could all meet. E-mail was an invaluable method for us to figure out convenient times. You could easily respond to other people's comments without having to voice-mail everyone on the team. It was also cheaper than a networked voice-mail service, which requires that everyone be on the same system, and you could check it from anywhere. When I had to leave for a few days, I checked my mail from home and was still contributing to the meetings, even though I was two hundred miles away.
>
> *College senior, twenty-one*

Beyond 'networking'

The rise of 'networking' (getting connected to lots of people) over the last two decades has been a direct response to the disappearance of traditional relationship opportunities. What makes so many people cringe when they think of 'networking' is when 'networking' seems totally fake. Often, there is no basis for networking relationships other than the fact that the people involved are willing to 'network' with each other – to learn each other's name and add each other's contact information to the phone card file. That doesn't give you very much to talk about.

▪ The embarrassment of one-sided relationships

One time, when I was still thinking in terms of 'networking,' I found out that I had a mutual friend with a guy who was rich and powerful (I'll call him Mr Q). I called up Mr Q and left a message with his secretary, leaving my name and the name of our mutual friend. Well our mutual friend must have carried some weight because I got a call back and an appointment to come and meet with Mr Q. I thought this was going to be great. Maybe we could be friends.

Throughout our meeting, Mr Q kept saying to me, 'What can I do for you?' And I kept saying, 'Nothing, really, thank you so much' and 'This is really a beautiful office' or whatever. We met for over an hour, but we had absolutely nothing to talk about. Finally, Mr Q stood up and said, 'Look, if you are a friend of [our mutual friend], I would be glad to help you. But, I am very busy and you will have to tell me what you want.' Wow. That was really, really embarrassing. After all, I didn't really want anything specific, I was just trying to 'network' with him. I thought we could be friends.

The punchline: *don't network for the sake of networking*. Don't pretend to have relationships with people whom you barely know. Don't waste people's time. Networking for the sake of networking is like crying wolf. Who has time for that? Wait until you have a good reason before pursuing a relationship with someone and then just do it.

▪ All relationships are transactional

Every relationship is an ongoing series of transactions. That's not good or bad, it's just the way it is. I call you. You call me back. We have dinner together. We enjoy each other's company. And we learn from each other just by talking. In fact, it sounds like you might be interested in the book I am reading, so I will give it to you when I am done. You realize that your friend does exactly what I need, so you offer to introduce us. Who knows, maybe there is some way you and I can work together too. (That's seven transactions, right there.) We are building a relationship. The more we transact, the more of a genuine basis we have for an authentic relationship.

> ❝ I knew that my loyalty to them and my commitment to work hard for them meant they would do anything in the world for me and that relationship would pay off over time. One of these days I was going to get them to help me. Every relationship will serve my purpose. I don't care if it's the janitor at the high school, I know that one of these days down the road that investing in that relationship is going to help me out. I want to know for myself that if I ever need them, people are going to want to go that extra mile for me.
>
> *Dairy Queen proprietor, also currently working a full-time job as a headhunter recruiting talented workers for pharmaceutical companies, twenty-nine*

■ Eleven strategies to connect with people who can help you

1. See relationships in terms of what you have to offer, instead of focusing on what you want or need to get

Even if you want or need to get something out of a relationship, it's more important to focus on what you can give. If you want lessons, you might think, 'I want someone to teach me,' but, instead, reframe it as 'I want to offer myself as a student.' If you want to teach, don't ask for students; rather, offer your skills and knowledge. Instead of asking to be introduced, offer someone the chance to introduce you. Instead of asking people to meet with each other, offer to bring people together.

> ❝ When you make it clear that you are offering something

instead of asking for something, most people are a whole lot more interested in pursuing a relationship with you.

World traveler, photography student, recently renovated a house, worked in a health food store for a while and also a coffee shop, twenty-five

Reframing relationships in terms of what you have to offer

Instead of . . .	Offer . . .
asking people to work for you	opportunities to work
asking to be hired	your time labor and creativity
asking for help	a chance to collaborate
demanding a great deal	to be a great customer
asking someone to buy	to sell
trying to get attention	to be engaging
wanting to be liked	to be likeable
asking to be introduced	someone the chance to introduce you
asking people to meet with each other	to bring people together

2. Identify and seek out the right decision makers

Every person is a decision maker; however, different people have decision making authority in different spheres. For example, the President of the United States may be the most powerful person in the world, but he has no power to decide what you are having for dinner – that is your decision. Likewise, you need to identify which decision makers have the power to make the decisions necessary for you to reach your goals.

First, make a list of every single decision which must be made for you to accomplish your goals: someone will have to make the decision to read your letter, to pass it on to the boss, to return your call, to have you in for an interview, to have you back for another interview, to review the other written materials you send along, to hire you as an employee or as a consultant, or to recommend you to another department, etc.

Second, next to every single decision on the list, identify the name and contact information of the person who has authority to make each decision. These are the decision makers you need to help you meet your goals.

Third, focus your relationship building on these decision makers. They are the people who can help you, right now.

> 66 I had been beating down this guy's door forever trying to get on this project team because he was a partner on the team and he was the guy I had a connection with. Later on I found out that I was totally wasting my time because he wasn't even in charge of staffing the project. I blew it by working on the wrong person.
>
> *Working in a big six accounting/management consulting firm, twenty-six*

3. Turn every new contact into a multiple contact

One of the most difficult things about reaching out and trying to form a relationship with a new person is just getting on that person's radar screen – getting noticed. It takes three to five contacts to get the average person to remember your name. If you are dealing with a very busy person, it takes five to seven contacts. How do you achieve multiple contacts without calling over and over and over again and seeming like a pest?

Simple – turn every new contact into a multiple contact. Never just call and leave a voice-mail at work. Never just leave a message on the answering machine at home. Never just overnight mail a package to the office. Never just send a personal letter to the home address. Never just fax a note. Never just e-mail. If you really want to make an impression, use all six methods of contact all at once whenever you reach out to a new person. It takes more time and effort, but that's one reason to do it: you can be sure it's not what everyone else is doing. I promise, you will get on the radar screen (like an incoming missile attack!). As long as you do all the contacts at once, you will not seem like a pest. But you will seem very thorough.

! *Caution: Imagine going to all that trouble, getting on the radar screen, and then having nothing to say, other than, 'No big deal, I just wanted to 'network' with you.' If you go to the trouble to get noticed by someone new, don't waste it (see page 93 on networking).*

❝ You have to beat people over the head to get noticed. I've left a dozen messages for the same person until he called back, but sometimes you also have to be creative. Just stop in to the office and see what the big delay is all about. But, don't seem like a fool. Don't come off like a pathetic girl with a crush if you don't know what to say when you finally get his attention.

Retail nomad, five stores and counting, twenty-four

4. Research before making contact

Before reaching out to make a new contact of any kind, do a little research (or a lot) about the people you are trying to reach, the company or organization, and the work they do. Do you know anyone else who already knows some of the people you are trying to contact? Or the organization? Or, at least the industry? Maybe that person could answer some questions for you? Are there any relevant articles or books you could read? Maybe the people you want to contact have published material of their own which you could find and read. Do the people have homepages? Does the company have a Web-site you can check out? Maybe you could call an organization, professional association, or government agency which could answer some questions. Or, you could make blind phone calls to someone's office before launching your contacts – call the person's assistant or co-worker without identifying yourself and ask a lot of questions. You'll be amazed at how much you can find out. (Hint: Just don't come across like a stalker.)

❝ I left my job in Hartford, and in Washington people were not even familiar with the firm I had worked for. But, when

I went to talk to people at Washington firms, I had all the right answers. From my experience in Hartford, I knew what information to check out, I knew how law firms run, and I knew what kind of information was available and how to get it. If you did not know what I did, you would have had to dig a lot deeper to get prepared or talk to someone like me who could give you the quick scoop and tell you where else to look.

Formerly director of legal recruiting at law firms in Connecticut and then Washington, DC, now back in Connecticut reinventing her career, twenty-nine

5. Use a mutual connection

Compare: first situation, I contact you out of the blue; second situation, I contact you and tell you that I know your friend (or your uncle or your boss or your sister or your customer or your former team mate or anyone else you know). In the second situation, I carry a lot more weight with you. Why? Because how you treat me may have implications for other relationships which matter to you. Just for the simple reason that there is a person out there in the world whom we both know and who matters to you.

First rule of mutual connections: make sure the relationship between the person you are trying to reach and your mutual connection is positive. Imagine this: I contact you and tell you that I know your old teacher (the one you most despised in high school) or your uncle (the one who always pinched you and called you names) or someone you went to college with (the one who dumped you after your second date). Sometimes it's better not to mention mutual connections, so always check.

Once you confirm your connection is positive, follow rule number two about using mutual connections: don't ask your mutual connection to make the introduction for you. Once you ask to be introduced, you will be paralyzed. You cannot go ahead and introduce yourself – you'll have to wait until your mutual connection gets around to introducing you. That may or may not happen, and even if it does, it is not likely to happen very soon. Moreover, you may be asking your mutual connection to do something he or she is not comfortable with for whatever reason (although he or she won't tell you that). You may be asking more than you realize.

Instead, tell your mutual connection that you are planning to reach out to the person you want to contact. Ask his or her advice; ask questions about the person, about his or her work, the best way to reach the person, the status of your mutual connection's relationship with the person. Then, simply ask if you can use your mutual connection's name when you reach out to the person you want to contact. By following rule two, you are actually doing your mutual connection a favor: you are giving him or her the chance to help both you and the person you want to reach without having to do anything, and you maintain control over the process.

Once you have a name to use, follow rule three: use the name shamelessly. For example, format your initial letters, faxes, and e-mails like this:

Date

Ms Person You Are Trying To Contact
99 Contact Drive
Contact City
AB1 2CD

    RE: Letter from mutual friend of Ms Mutual Friend

Dear Ms. Contact:

Body of the letter.

                Sincerely,
                You

cc: Ms Mutual Friend

Then actually send copies of every communication to your mutual connection. He or she can always toss away the copies you send, but by keeping your mutual connection in the loop you will be demonstrating respect and recognition for lending you the use of his or her name. The person you are contacting will also be more conscientious in dealing with you because he or she will feel a greater sense of account-ability about the relationship.

> 66 I spent most of my time during my internship developing a relationship with this guy, who later became the publisher. After my internship, I left the flagship publication and worked for a smaller niche publication, but I stayed in touch. Later, I was able to make my way back to the flagship magazine because whenever there were changes, I was staying in touch with everyone. I made sure it was known that the publisher was in my corner. I was able to use his name freely. That helped when there was a new managing editor: I got back on staff.
>
> *Parlayed unpaid placement into position as associate editor*
> *at a newsstand magazine, twenty-six*

6. Make your communiqués interesting and useful

Demonstrate your value by making the materials you send interesting and useful. Send an article you think might be of interest to the person you are contacting, or an article mentioning the person or mentioning yourself. Go one step further – write an article about the subject matter of your contact, get it published anywhere, and send that along. Or just send a copy of the unpublished article. Do a little research and dig up a useful piece of information to share. Paint a picture. Create a spreadsheet. Send charts and graphs. Send a ten-minute infomercial. Direct the person to your personal homepage. Create a life-size poster of yourself holding out your CV. Or a new logo for the person's business. Or a prototype of the new product you are inventing. You'll think of something. Just make certain whatever you do is in good taste.

> 66 I actually put my résumé on a T-shirt and sent it to the CEO (at Nike). I also put my résumé on a note in a Perrier bottle and sent that one to the CEO there saying, 'Help, I am a

marketing genius trapped in the body of an MBA.' You
have to be creative without going overboard.
Doing special industry research at an investment bank,
twenty-nine

7. Identify and win over gatekeepers

Even if you do everything right, the person you want to reach
may never even know you exist. Why? Gatekeepers. Many of
the people you want to reach will be insulated from the
outside world by assistants who carefully guard their time
and attention. These assistants screen voice-mail, e-mail,
paper mail, faxes, overnight packages, and any other communications before their bosses ever see them. That makes
gatekeepers very powerful. And they have a strong personal
incentive for keeping other ambitious people away from their
bosses: who needs more competition? No matter how many
times you call, write, fax, e-mail, and courier, if the gatekeeper
doesn't want you to get through, you probably won't.

But gatekeepers are people too. And if you want their help,
you have to recognize them as individuals and take the time
to build relationships with them.

First, identify the real gatekeeper by asking good questions:
'Do you check Ms Jones's voice-mail or does she check it
herself?' Or, 'Do you keep Mr Smith's schedule or does he
keep it himself?' Or, 'If I send Ms Jones a fax, would you be
the person who would see it first?'

Once you have identified the real gatekeeper, treat that
person with the same measure of respect and deference you
would accord the decision maker you are trying to reach.

Teach the gatekeeper your name by using multiple contacts
addressed directly to the gatekeeper: send a letter, voice-mail,
fax, and e-mail, all at the same time thanking the gatekeeper
for taking the time to talk with you. Don't even mention the
decision maker in this round of communication.

Follow up with a phone call and see if the gatekeeper

remembers you. If so, then it's time to ask the gatekeeper to raise the gate and let you in: 'What would be the best way to get a fax directly to Ms Jones?' 'How could I make sure that Mr Smith will get my letter?' When you win over the gatekeeper, you will get past the gate.

> **"** I've been an assistant before, so I know how it works. Win over the assistant and you've got it made.
>> *Temp, used to work as administrative assistant, also taking graduate courses in business, twenty-five*

8. Once you get on the radar screen, prove that you are more than a blip

Getting noticed is not enough. How do you get decision makers to stop and pay attention to you? You have to make it clear that you are offering to add value: 'This is exactly what, where, when, why, and how I am offering to add value.' Of course, if you sell it, be prepared to deliver.

The second way to get a decision maker to pay attention is to set up a series of commitments with concrete deadlines and build an instant track record of reliability by keeping the commitments you make. These commitments can be minor ('I will call you on Thursday at 10.00 a.m.' or 'I'll look into that and get back to you by the end of the week') as long as they are specific and you complete them as promised.

Your best strategy: commit to making a concrete proposal by a certain deadline, then deliver. If your first proposal does not get accepted, don't give up. Maybe the decision maker you are contacting will suggest an approach to revising the proposal. Then revise away. Keep proving yourself over and over again. Eventually, it will pay off.

> **"** Once you prove you are one of the people who delivers on what she promises, you become a whole lot more valuable. That's when everybody wants to get you involved in their project.
>> *Scientist turned high school teacher, twenty-eight*

9. Become Ms or Mr Follow-up

Once you get the ball rolling, don't be the one to let it drop. Always follow up. If a relationship is hot (you just submitted a proposal), then your follow-ups should be frequent (once a week). If a relationship isn't going anywhere right away (like the person said, 'I'll get back to you if I am interested'), then your follow-ups should be less frequent (every other month). If you are not sure, then ask, 'When is the best time for me to follow up next?' If the person says, 'Get lost,' then don't call back. If she or he says, 'Why don't you call me in about four weeks,' then confirm a specific date and time and tell the person you are writing the appointment in your calendar. If he or she says, 'You don't have to follow up, I will call you in a few weeks,' then let the person know that if you haven't heard from him or her by a certain date, you will make sure to follow up.

Bear in mind, if you are reaching out and trying to build relationships with a lot of people, you are going to have a lot of follow-ups to make and they are going to be scheduled sometimes months in advance. That means you need a system for keeping track of your follow-ups, so you won't forget. Keeping a calendar or schedule is very effective, but only if you check it every day. There is plenty of scheduling software available which will give you a reminder automatically if you have an appointment scheduled, but that means you have to use the software and keep your computer on. Some people keep a running list in their pocket. Whatever. Just don't drop the ball.

> 66 I make base plus commission, so I can't afford to have a customer come in, look around, and leave without buying. I keep a schedule of follow-ups with my potential customers and I call to check in and offer my service about once a month. That's it. But, it works. When they are ready, they come to me, instead of someone else.
>
> *Selling used cars, twenty-four*

10. Keep your contact information up-to-date and keep others up-to-date with your contact information

People move around a lot these days, so it takes a little more effort to stay in touch. You'll need to maintain good records with the contact information of the people with whom you are building relationships. Whether you use database software or an old-fashioned notebook, use your contact information (paper mail and e-mail addresses, phone and fax numbers) at least twice a year, so you can verify which information remains current and update information as it changes.

Also make sure that your own most current contact information is always available to people who want to stay in touch with you. If you are really on the move, think about getting a semipermanent post office box or voice message service in addition to your e-mail address so that people don't have to struggle to stay in touch with you. Whenever you do move and your contact information changes, let everyone in your contact universe know at least twice: send a postcard, leave voice-mail, send a fax, and an e-mail. Twice.

> **❝** I have moved four times in the last three years. I would be a missing person if I were not so meticulous about sending out change-of-address cards.
>
> *Traveler, twenty-five*

11. Take personal responsibility for maintaining the positive energy in relationships

There are eight simple rules for maintaining positive energy in any relationship:

1. *Make yourself a model of trustworthiness:* Be honest, realistic, responsible, on time and reliable, be accountable, and never make excuses when you make a mistake (just apologize and then fix it).

2. *Remove your ego:* Don't take yourself too seriously, but always take your work seriously; extend personal vulnerability, but never undermine your own credibility.

3. *Listen with your eyes and ears wide open:* Do not interrupt; ask open-ended questions first, and only after listening to the answers ask pointed clarifying questions; respond directly to what the other person says.

4. *Empathize:* Try to imagine yourself in the other person's position; ask yourself what thoughts and feelings you would have if you were the other person.

5. *Be respectful and kind:* Take courtesy the extra mile. If you think the other person is pressed for time, be brief; if you think something is wrong, ask if there is anything you can do to help.

6. *Speak up:* If you don't say what you are thinking and feeling, the other person won't know (unless he or she can read your mind, in which case you are in trouble anyway).

7. *Be a motivator:* Visualize positive results; be enthusiastic and share your positive vision; never speak of a problem unless you have thought of at least one potential solution.

8. *Celebrate the success of others:* Always give people credit for their achievements, no matter how small; and try to catch people doing things right.

If you reach out to people with the effective strategies outlined in this chapter, you will build strong connections with decision makers who can help you. Invest the time and energy it takes to build long-term relationships with these people. Over time, these relationships will become authentic and deep. These people will be your anchors in our chaotic world (and you may become an anchor for someone else). You will provide each other with support and security. These relationships have the potential to become the most reliable institutions in your life.

Maximizing relationship opportunities

Chapter 6

■ Shifting relationships and overlapping roles

In today's world, relationships constantly shift and overlap. The person who is your boss today might be your subordinate tomorrow, a member of your project team the next day, and your boss again the following week. The person who is buying something from you today may be selling you something else tomorrow. You may find yourself teaching a person who has taught you a lot some time in the past. Maybe this year you will work side by side with someone and then next year that person will become your adversary.

How do you maximize relationships which are constantly shifting? First, be aware of the changing roles people play in your life: family, friend, cohort, adversary, boss, subordinate, teammate, vendor, customer/client, teacher, student, etc. Clarify the roles different people are playing in your life at any given time. Second, don't let relationships just happen to you; actively shape meaningful and gratifying roles for yourself in the lives of others.

■ Nine ways to get the most out of the relationships you cultivate

1. Don't be afraid to ask family and friends for help

Your family and friends are your primary support network in life – invest in them wisely. These relationships are based on love, fondness, common attachments, and the bonds of time. Within these relationships, you give unconditionally and you hope to receive unconditionally. Of course, plenty of 'favors' occur among family and friends (and not without complications and problems). However, you do things for your family and friends just because you love them or you like them. But how often do they ask for your help?

Some people are hesitant to ask their family and friends for help – somehow, to them, it seems like 'cheating.' Here is why it is not: if you don't seek help from people you already know, you have to find people you don't know to help you. But first you'll have to get to know them, so you might as well start with the people you already know.

Some people are hesitant to ask family and friends for help because they are afraid they will be imposing. You may be imposing, if you don't look at help as a mutual arrangement.

Make a list of all the family and friends in your life whom you would gladly help in any way you are able. Think of all the different ways you could help and be generous with each person on your list. Then, give your help generously and give it unconditionally.

The family members and friends you are happy to help generously and unconditionally are the same ones who will probably be happy to help you. Take that same list and alongside the notations you have made of what you have to offer each person, make a note of all the ways each person can help you (keeping in mind each person's scope of authority and influence). When you need their help, don't be afraid to ask for it.

> ❝ How many real friends do we go through life with? It's important for me to stay in touch with my old friends. I like to just be myself and try to laugh as much as possible, try not to take myself too seriously. And old friends are the only people I can really do that with. Those people are like family. They are there for me whenever I need them.
>
> *City councillor in one of America's largest cities, twenty-nine*

2. Volunteer to work with others on a shared goal

Whatever team effort you choose, giving your time along with other people in pursuit of a shared purpose is a very powerful experience. You learn from creating a shared mission, making mutual commitments, working in tandem, and temporarily subordinating your own interests to the interests of a group. You learn about service, teamwork and commitment. You learn to rely on people and to be reliable. You learn interdependence. And you will learn other valuable skills that you might not learn without volunteering. What is more, you will form deep bonds with your teammates and some of them may become your best friends.

If there is a particular cause that excites you – the environment, the national debt, education, AIDS, transport, organized labor, charity, religion, an election campaign – that's great. Get involved in a team effort to do something about it. Or do something that has nothing to do with a cause – like a soccer league, a chess club, a reading group/learning circle, a karate school, or a social club for the experience of working together with others on a shared goal.

Once you find the right team, be one of the most valuable players. At first, go in and just do what they say. When you have been volunteering long enough to know what's going on, start thinking of the best ways you can be valuable to the organization. If it's something new, write a proposal and give it to the head of the organization, offering to implement your idea.

If there is no group effort dedicated to your cause (or at least no good ones), then start your own organization to serve the cause better. Recruit a core group, brainstorm your mission, set clear goals, divide responsibility, and get to work.

❝ We set up the Princeton Women's Network as a way to get a bunch of women together to do a community service project and to work with an organization that provides mentoring and job skills for women coming out of job-training programs. We got mailing labels through the alumni council of the university for everyone in New York City, where we were. We sent out about a thousand little flyers. Eighty people showed up for a meeting and another hundred called and said they couldn't come but thought it was a great idea. The original project itself didn't work out, but the idea took off of having a women's network that would help everyone stay in touch. Because Princeton didn't go coed until 1970, just about all the women in the

Be a part of a team

Brainstorm for a while about what kind of team activity you would most enjoy. There are a million possibilities. Let me throw out a few:

▷ Play in a sports league or be a coach.

▷ Be a business manager for a team or an organization.

▷ Volunteer for a political campaign or a charity.

▷ Run for office yourself or work for a political action committee.

▷ Attend a house of worship or become active in your religious community.

▷ Join a business or professional association.

▷ Organize a charity fundraising event.

▷ Start a club around any interest (games, food, reading, languages, music, exercise).

▷ Join a club that already exists.

▷ Take part in on-line chat groups.

▷ Take a class or enroll in school.

▷ Form a learning circle with some friends (create a learning agenda and decide on materials, meet regularly for discussions, or communicate with each other by e-mail and in chat groups).

▷ Join a union.

▷ Start a small business or a full-blown business with a couple of partners.

▷ Seek out team projects at work or propose projects at work which require a team (offer to recruit the team and maybe even to be the team facilitator).

organization are relatively young in their twenties and thirties. We do community service projects, professional development workshops, book groups, there is a small business group, a women and architecture group, and one for women and science, and we send out three newsletters a year. I have learned a ton. One of the women I met is a money manager who just started her own mutual fund and she asked me to be on the board. The only reason she asked me is because she got involved and we were involved in the same organization together, working for the same things.

Turned a two year appointment as a research assistant in a prestigious foundation into four years and counting by reinventing her job as often as she has to, twenty-seven

3. Bring together people with mutual interests

Just as you value the opportunity to develop relationships with people who share your interests, you probably know plenty of people who don't know each other but could benefit from being introduced. You can do some of those people a big favor just by being the one to introduce them. If you do that whenever you can, people will start returning the favor.

In theory, there are only six degrees of separation between me or you and anyone else in the world. Each 'somebody' is one link in that chain of relationships. You can be a key link in the chain of a lot of relationships by bringing people together.

Make a list of family, friends, co-workers, customers, vendors, and other reasonably close acquaintances. Go back over the list and make some notes about each person, his or her needs, wants, interests, and work. Try pairing people up on paper – people you think you might want to introduce. Look for pairs who seem to have things in common or that are com- plimentary. Ask if they would like to meet each other. Once you make the connection for people, you can back off and leave the relationship to them. Or maybe there is a project you could all work on together as a team. At least, you could all pal around together sometimes.

❝ The internship with the Fish and Wildlife Service was in the same area as my internship with the state Department of Environmental Management, and I thought that the two groups should talk and work together. I got my supervisor from the state internship talking with my supervisor and her superiors at Fish and Wildlife. I set up a meeting and then we had a couple more meetings and we talked about what could be done together and ideas just flowed from that. As a result, we started an outreach program and a volunteer program. And we helped protect an endangered species of insect. None of that would have happened if my two supervisors had never just talked, so I was glad I introduced them.

First-year graduate student in forestry after two years of balancing placements, retail jobs, and graduate courses, twenty-four

4. Give subordinates the power to excel

Being able to bring out the best in people is a very valuable skill, and the only way to develop that skill is to practice it. If you practice empowering people and giving them room to excel, they will do their best work and that will add value directly to the bottom line. Those you manage will be genuinely grateful to you for helping them succeed and they will want to work harder for you. And remember, your subordinate today may be your boss tomorrow or your team leader or your teacher, supplier, customer, client, etc. So invest in relationships with all of your subordinates by being an empowering manager.

❝ If you are a good manager, people are going to remember that. You remember people who are good to you at work. If you are an asshole, just wait until I come in here as a customer myself or have a chance to bust on you. You want to be one of those managers people remember really liking, not because you are really easy, but because you care.

College senior juggling placements and retail jobs, twenty-two

To empower those you manage effectively, apply four basic principles:

▷ *Give people the resources to orient and train themselves.* Set concrete learning goals with clear deadlines. Provide massive amounts of information in every format available – books, journals, magazine articles, old files, audio, video, CD-ROM, CD-interactive, on-line resources. Then give them the remote control and let them learn. Insist that those you manage treat learning as a core business task.

▷ *Teach people to micromanage themselves.* People need to have a daily sense of accomplishment to stay focused and motivated; however, many people find themselves working on big projects where the major goals are achieved only after months or years, not days. Some people have a hard time appreciating the tangible results of their work. Others just don't think in terms of concrete goals. Help those whom you manage to understand their tasks and responsibilities in bite-size chunks which they can keep track of from day to day.

For example, you would teach a sales representative to carve up the job into these chunks: adding names to a leads list; making initial phone calls; sending follow-up notes; making follow up phone calls; scheduling appointments; making presentations in person; creating proposals; closing deals; supervising delivery and ensuring good customer service; staying in contact for repeat business.

Once you teach employees to carve up their jobs into bite-size chunks, they have more power to set their own concrete goals in each category and monitor their own achievement from day to day.

▷ *Provide FAST – frequent, accurate, specific, and timely – feedback.* Don't make people wonder how they are doing or wait for six-month or twelve-month reviews which are often inaccurate, vague, and moot. Give them feedback which helps them improve – do more of what they are doing right and correct what they are doing wrong.

▷ *Confer proper credit, recognition, and reward.* If you have followed the first three principles, then those you manage will be aggressively training themselves; micromanaging their own work; setting concrete goals each day and monitoring their own day-to-day productivity; and receiving the kind of FAST feedback which helps them constantly improve. Thus, you will have created the perfect conditions for giving employees the rewards they most desire: increases in responsibility and creative freedom, and ever more flexible work schedules. Other favored rewards for a job well done: public recognition, awards, vacation or personal time, and increases in pay.

5. Manage your boss in a way that gives you room to excel

Your most valuable career capital is your time, labor, and creativity. Whenever you are working, you are investing that capital. Maximize your investment. Pursue your work goals in a way that allows you to learn and grow; build new skills and perform diverse tasks; achieve tangible results and collect proof of your value in the workplace; receive recognition, credit, and rewards; maintain balance between your working life and non-working life; and build relationships with lots of people who can help you.

Work closely with good managers: make the most of the learning opportunities they provide; get them to help you formulate ambitious goals and determine realistic deadlines; pay close attention to the feedback they provide; appreciate the recognition, credit and rewards they provide; and never stop earning the responsibility, creative freedom, and flexibility they want to provide for you. The best managers are leaders, role models, teachers, coaches and mentors; they go to bat for anyone who works hard for them. You will never forget them and they will never forget you; they may become some of the best friends you ever have.

Bad managers, however, are a whole different story. No matter how miserable they may be, you cannot let them stand in your way. Remember, your boss is only your boss for today – tomorrow, he or she could be your customer, your supplier, teammate, subordinate, friend, adversary, teacher, student, spouse, in-law, or somebody you never see again. The hierarchy of your relationship is temporary. If your manager is getting in your way, you must take control of the situation.

> ❝ The thing you have to do with a shitty manager is turn it around. I call it 'managing up.' There are ways you can work around your boss and make stuff happen despite the boss. You take responsibility for the situation and just run with it.
>
> *Sales representative for a consumer products company, formerly a sales representative for a different company, twenty-six*

Let me recommend some techniques for dealing with the five most common bad management syndromes you are likely to face in the workplace:

Syndrome 1: The boss fails to provide adequate training resources.

Remedy

Ask the boss to make a list of all the skills and knowledge he or she expects you to know to be able to perform your current tasks and meet your current responsibilities. Treat this list as your learning agenda.

Return a copy of this learning agenda, and this time ask the boss to indicate the best resources for learning all the different skills and knowledge you are expected to learn (books, journals, articles, audio, video, CD, old files, hands-on experience, coaching by an expert, or whatever).

Meanwhile, discuss your learning agenda with as many knowledgeable people as you can, especially people who have done the kind of work you will be doing. Get them to recommend learning resources too.

Compare the learning resources recommended by your boss with those recommended by the other people you have consulted. Prepare your own list of learning resources. Next, create a learning plan based on the agenda your boss helped you create and the list of necessary learning resources you have prepared. Set concrete learning goals. Establish clear deadlines for achieving each goal. List all of the resources you will need. Create a timeline and mark the first point on the timeline with this goal 'Obtain all learning resources from (boss).' Submit the learning plan for your boss's approval.

Syndrome 2: The boss wastes a lot of your time.

Remedy

Make it clear that you are not selling your time. You are selling your work, creativity, and results. While you are totally committed to achieving concrete results by clear deadlines, your time still belongs to you. That means face time (being at work late just to be there) is out. Since bad planning causes false urgency, focus your boss's attention on planning your time. That way, you won't sit around all day waiting for your boss to get around to telling you that something needs to be done by first thing the next morning.

Insist on a clear statement of the tangible results expected of you: 'Exactly what do you want to be holding in your hands when I am done?' By saying this, you remind your manager that you are there to add value, to sell your creative output, and you demonstrate that it is worthwhile for your manager to spend a small amount of time planning in order to facilitate your productivity.

Insist on clear deadlines, no matter how small or how large

the stated goal of the assignment. If the result is too minuscule to justify a deadline, then your manager is not delegating enough responsibility. If the result seems too large to set a realistic deadline, then it is not sufficiently concrete. By insisting on clear deadlines, you require your manager to clarify the ownership of goals. In doing so, you help map out the terrain in which you can increase your autonomy and gain more control over your schedule.

If your manager interrupts you between goal-setting and deadline with a new goal, remind your manager of the old goal and deadline. Explain that you will have to renegotiate the deadline for goal number one or else build in more time to achieve goal number two.

Syndrome 3: The boss tries to be intimidating, loud, mean, or abusive.

Remedy

Remember, this is his or her psychological problem, not yours. Document all abuse and all of the solutions you attempt to end the abuse by keeping a notepad with dates and times and names and concrete examples. Seek support among your colleagues (and family and friends), while trying to avoid your abusive boss. After you have compiled a decent record of the abuse, engage your manager in a private confrontation about the problem and propose 'setting guidelines for a more professional relationship.' You are also entitled to report your abusive boss to senior management if discussing it does not work. In some cases, senior management will have a legal obligation to take action. Depending on the circumstances, you may need to go over your manager's head immediately – if so, explain the situation to a senior person and propose your solution. If you cannot resolve the problem through internal channels, you may need to consult a solicitor about taking legal action.

Syndrome 4: The boss is a micromanager.

Remedy

Untangle yourself firmly but gently. At the outset of any assignment, insist on putting in the up-front time with your manager to divide up all the concrete results which need to be produced. Get it clear: which results are your responsibility? Which belong to someone else?

Demand a concrete deadline for every single result which is your responsibility. Always set a day and time for your next meeting with your micromanager. Whenever your manager tries to get tangled up in your work, remind him or her of the concrete results which are your responsibility, your deadline, and the meeting you already have scheduled to review. Then say, 'I'll make a note of that issue so we can add it to our discussion when we meet next.' And keep a notebook with all of those notations.

Syndrome 5: The boss offers no feedback, credit, or reward.

Remedy

Collect evidence, all the time, of the quality and productivity of your work. The best evidence is FAST feedback from your manager. If you're not getting FAST feedback from your manager, generate your own. Set realistic goals (long-term, intermediate, and short-term) for yourself in every category of your job and monitor your progress. Before you can set realistic goals, you have to make a list of every little piece of your particular job and think about what it means to accomplish each piece as well as you possibly can. Spend a week writing down every single thing you do. Figure out how long it takes to get each thing done so you will be able thereafter to schedule time for the accomplishment of each goal.

Break down each of your goals into little minigoals that take two or three hours each so you will be able to tell right along whether you are keeping up with your schedule. As you accomplish each minigoal, make a note on your schedule. This will become your own ongoing record of the value you add hour by hour, every day, and the lasting proof of your value as an employee in any workplace.

If a manager has stolen credit for your work, especially if it is a chronic problem, the best remedy is a little sunlight – expose the thief. Let several people at several levels know that the work in question was done by you. And try to include some proof that you did the work (like an earlier draft). They will figure out the rest.

The best medicine, however, is often prevention. At the beginning of any assignment, define up front which results are your responsibility. Then let your manager know that you are going to take the hit, personally, for whatever goes wrong. On the flip side, you can make sure to point out that you are going to do a great job because you know this is a great opportunity for you to shine. By the way, try to do this publicly, in writing if you can, and let multiple people know about this division of responsibility and ownership of results. Also, whenever possible, make sure to keep senior people in that loop. They will be impressed and you will be covered.

6. Develop a total customer service mindset

Treat everyone you deal with as a customer – co-workers, employees, managers, suppliers, service people, and actual customers. Customer service is what keeps your customers coming back for more. Just as important, good customer service gets people recommending you to others. On average, every satisfied customer will tell one other person every time they have a positive customer service experience. Word of mouth is the least expensive and most effective marketing tool of all.

But it works both ways: pissed-off customers tell an average of nine people every time they have a bad customer service experience. Do the sums: you have to impress nine customers for every one you piss off, just to break even. Never forget, it's not just the quality of what you have to offer that matters. Customer service is all about how you offer and how you deliver and how you follow-up. Dazzle everyone you deal with by applying these nine principles of customer service:

▷ Identify the customer's needs before doing anything else. Say, 'Please tell me what I can do to help you' and then listen very carefully. Sometimes customers don't know exactly what their needs are. In that case, the first thing you can help them do is figure out their needs.

▷ Once you identify the customer's needs, make their needs your first priority.

▷ Always be honest and accurate. For example, if you are on the phone, don't ever say, 'Would you please hold on for a second?' That's a lie. It's always going to be more than a second, and your customer is going to be frustrated. If it's going to be two or three minutes then say it. Convey honesty and accuracy in everything you do, no matter how minuscule it may seem.

▷ Never say, 'I can't help you with that' or 'We don't do that' or 'We don't sell that.' Instead, say, 'Let me figure out a way to help you' or 'Let me find someone who can do that for you' or 'who can sell you that.'

▷ Always be on time. Give yourself more time up front, instead of being late in the end. If it looks like you may be late, warn your customer in plenty of time, so he or she can plan for the new deadline, but work around the clock for days if necessary to meet your original deadline.

▷ Never keep a customer waiting.

▷ Instead of making customers come to you, always go to them.

▷ Remember, you don't need a reason to meet a customer's needs. Never ask 'Why?' Just ask 'Is that all you need from me right now or is there something else I can do for you?'

▷ Always follow up after the fact. Ask your customer if he or she was satisfied with the quality of what and how, if there was anything you could have done better, and if there is anything else you can do now.

> **❝** Generally the consumer is always right. There are certain people who will buy anything and there are people who will quibble over five dollars. You have to make them feel like they have been successful in whatever they are trying to do. That's what makes them come back to the store again. Sometimes people know what they want and sometimes you have to really ask them questions and help them figure out what they are looking for. You have to really know how to read what people want you to be and modify your behavior toward what they want. You learn how to understand people's needs and leave them feeling good about the experience.
>
> *Six year veteran at The Gap (often balancing other retail jobs)*
> *and currently in graduate school studying speech pathology,*
> *twenty-three*

7. Become a great customer

Some people think of being a customer as if they are in an adversarial position. They are always worried about getting the bad side of a bargain. In the back of their minds, they think about all the remedies that might be available in the event they feel disappointed or cheated in a particular transaction – like complaining to the Office of Fair Trading, going to the small claims court, reporting an employee to the owner, writing a letter to the editor of the local newspaper, telling anyone who will listen, or standing in front of the store with a big sign saying DON'T SHOP HERE. While all of these remedies are available to an aggrieved customer, none will help you be the kind of customer who routinely gets your needs met at a low cost and with little hassle. Who wants to have Ralph Nader as a customer? Even if you win every consumer skirmish you get involved in, you are missing some tremendous relationship opportunities.

Think about it: people are very eager to spend time with and strengthen their connections with customers and potential customers. It's inevitable, in a free market system, that you are going to be somebody's customer. Why be any old customer when you can be a great customer? Great customers get all the best deals, the free samples, the speedy deliveries, the emergency rush jobs on a weekend. Why? Because great customers have a lot to offer: repeat business, positive word of mouth, business referrals, comfort, ease and trust in dealings. And who knows? The person selling you something today could be your customer tomorrow, or your boss, or your teacher, etc.

Let me suggest six ways you can become a great customer:

▷ Be very clear about your own wants and needs. What do you want? When? Where? How? Why? Set priorities: is it more important that you get good quality merchandise or that you be treated like a VIP? Maybe you need both. Would you rather have someone who can meet your needs overnight or that you deal with someone who is right around the corner from your home? Maybe you need both. How important is price? And so on.

▷ Identify the potential vendors who can meet your needs. Get clear information about each of them. Make a decision: choose the vendor you'd really like to deal with. And, always have a back-up: who is your second choice if the first one doesn't work out or if the first one can't meet your needs sometime for some reason?

▷ Over the course of your first few dealings, get to know the people. Find out how the place operates. Get comfortable.

▷ Let them know that you have chosen them carefully, over the competition, because you feel they are the best. Let them know you plan to be a great customer: Give them repeat business, tell people about them, refer people to them, and be easy and comfortable to deal with.

▷ Let them know about your needs in no uncertain terms. And, let them know that you are counting on them to meet your needs. 'The reason I would never go to anyone else is that I know you care about my needs and are willing to meet them.'

▷ Treat everyone with respect and courtesy. Give clear recognition and appreciation for good service, and deal with mistakes and problems without losing your temper.

> ❝ Do the nicest customers definitely get the best service? I mean, I usually don't spit in your coffee even if you're an asshole. But come in every day with a smile on your face and give me generous tips and I probably won't even charge you for a cup of coffee.
>
> *Coffee shop clerk, twenty-four*

8. Be the diligent protégé of a worthy mentor

There is no relationship more valuable to an aspiring person than being the diligent protégé of a worthy mentor. Studying the example of an accomplished, experienced, and wise person whom you admire will teach you so much about the world and about yourself. Having a mentor means having someone you can imitate; who will teach you and share experiences with you; who will answer your deepest questions, push you and demand more of you than you demand of yourself; who believes you are capable of achieving the impossible and is willing to help you do it; who will provide you with unique opportunities to prove yourself; introduce you to others; value your opinions and ideas, seek your input and learn from you; like you, care about you, and even love you. Having a mentor is the greatest, but you can't have one until you are ready to open up and learn.

Where do you find a mentor? It depends on what you want to

learn, but find someone experienced, accomplished, and wise, whom you know reasonably well, respect and would like to emulate: maybe an aunt, uncle, sibling, cousin, co-worker, boss, customer, vendor, teacher, professor, coach, tutor, or community leader. If a would-be-mentor appears out of the clear blue sky, just make sure you get to know the person pretty well before taking his or her advice on anything important.

> **❝** I finally met someone who was a mentor to me: he was doing the work I am interested in doing. I spent a lot of time with him because he was my supervisor in my internship and he was willing to teach me. I was definitely willing to learn. He told me a lot about the realities of dealing with people . . . and people's perceptions of the kind of work we were doing. He was encouraging. He knew what he was doing. Just being around him was helpful. Seeing how much he cared. . . . And he even helped me to choose schools to apply to and pick out classes when I went to graduate school.
>
> *Forestry graduate student, formerly balancing several placements, twenty-four*

9. Be a mentor

Be a mentor to someone less experienced than yourself. Being a mentor, and role model, keeps you on your toes. If someone young and impressionable is imitating your example, there is a lot of pressure to always be at your very best. Teaching someone the basics of anything keeps the basics present and fresh in your daily routine. No matter how sophisticated you may become in any field of knowledge, you never want to stray too far from the basics.

In seeking to explain a complex problem to a beginner, you will often think of new ways of looking at the problem, and maybe find a new solution. Plus, helping another person learn and grow is empowering because it reminds you of how much learning and growing there is in your own past, present, and future. It's also gratifying to help someone

Empty your cup

Let me tell you a karate story: 'There was a young karate student who practiced very hard and was very skilled. When his teacher died, he searched and searched, until he finally found a new master he wanted to study with. He went to ask the master to accept him as a new student. The young student tried to impress the master by performing everything he knew. He showed off his best skills, his finest techniques, almost every trick he had in his repertoire, in the hope of convincing the master to accept him as a student. After hours of watching the young student perform, the master invited the student to sit down for a cup of tea. The master set out two tea cups, filled his own first and then began pouring tea into the student's cup. The tea ran over the top of the student's cup and the master kept pouring until the tea ran over onto the table and all over the floor. The student jumped to his feet and exclaimed 'My cup is too full. My cup is too full.' The master said, 'Yes. Your cup is too full. Come back when your cup is empty. Then you will have room for my teachings."

you care about. And having a protégé forces you to practice your leadership skills – priority setting, communication, and motivation.

Find an appropriate protégé who wants a mentor: maybe you have a sibling, niece, nephew, cousin, co-worker, team-member, subordinate, student, friend, sibling of a friend, customer, vendor, or just someone who drops out of the clear blue sky. Set a good example. Share your knowledge and skills. Provide your would-be protégé with unique opportunities to prove him- or herself. Spend the time. Be aware of your role and live up to it.

> ❝ I always felt that something as small as an hour or two of my time devoted to one student was worth [it]. I had a student who was failing her first two classes in the morning because she kept 'missing her bus.' I told her she had better be ready on time for the rest of the year because I was her ride to school from now on, and she was not allowed to make me late! I picked her up every morning, and she worked on her homework in my office after school every day.
>
> *Former physical education teacher, athletic trainer, personal trainer, and bartender, currently a sales representative, thirty*

Every day of your life you will have opportunities to maximize relationships with people playing all kinds of shifting and overlapping roles in your life. Don't let these opportunities escape you. Invigorating your existing relationships and cultivating new ones will enrich your life experience, provide you with invaluable support in times of trouble, and a warm feeling of security when things are going well.

Becoming a day-to-day value adder

Those of us in our twenties today are likely to do all of the following before we turn thirty: work in one pretty good job, one pretty bad job, drop out of the rat race for a while, start a business, and at least think about going back to school. Often, we'll be doing several of these things at once.

Every single year, millions of us under the age of thirty-four change jobs. Why? Are we all just restless? What are we searching for?

Perhaps most of us are searching for success and security. The problem is that it seems as if none of us knows what success and security is supposed to look like for our generation.

> ❝ I got a job selling stationary and art supplies and that lasted a year but once I memorized all the stock numbers, the job got very boring. After that I got a job as a carpenter through a friend who agreed to teach me the ropes, and that was cool, and great fun, and I did that for a year and a half. Then I moved back to my parents' place in Pennsylvania and I started doing sculpture again and photography. After that I set up my jewelry studio in the basement of my parents' house. I sold some of it at a local craft shop, where I got a job working part-time, but it was just sort of pocket change. I decided to remodel a small barn into an apartment, and that took a lot of my creative energy. At the same time I was teaching this course at the local university. Now I live in California working at a very high-tech company.
>
> *Artist, craftsman, photographer, former university instructor, computer graphics designer, thirty-one*

> ❝ I am always a step ahead. Before I got fired, on the quiet side, I started faxing out my résumé to different companies. I went on an interview at First USA Bank, and I got hired. But I was out of work for two or three weeks before I went into the training program at the bank.
>
> *College senior balancing placements and several part-time jobs, twenty-two*

> ❝ In college I was not very career-oriented at all. I kind of fell into tutoring and chemistry and stuff, but I definitely saw

myself as the Nobel Prize-winning scientist or something like that. Then I went to graduate school – the next anointed career path for me. I got into Cal Tech and it was total hell. I realized that I didn't like doing the things I thought I should like doing, like working in the laboratory all by myself – it was teaching that I do enjoy and I found I'm pretty good at it.

Scientist, high school teacher, currently getting her second
masters degree, twenty-eight

❝ There's no way I am going to stay here more than a couple of years but I am not going to tell them that. This job serves my purpose right now. I am going to do what I can with it and then probably go back to school.

Working in an advertising firm, first as an internal messenger,
now as an account assistant, twenty-four

In today's world, searching for success and security is like searching for destinations in Atlantis: all the paths are washed out and all the road maps are obsolete. Those starting out our careers in the post-jobs era must remap our way to security, picking up the bits and pieces of success in one new experience after another. That process of remapping is what I call 'self-building': building ourselves in each new experience with the sudden rush of new skills, new relationships, and new creative opportunities. And when the self-building dividends of one new experience begin to slow down, we move on to a brand-new experience, or create a new experience right where we are in our current workplace, or diversify by juggling several experiences at once.

Unlike those of prior generations, successful people in our generation see risk in long-term investments, and security in successive short-term investments of time, labor and creativity. However, the inclination to search for success and security by moving from one new experience to the next is in perfect sync with the changing nature of work: today, it is nearly impossible to draw clear boundaries around the work being done by most of those adding value in the workforce. The labor market is fluid, scattered, and unpredictable. Work is about meeting immediate and ephemeral needs, whether you work as a temp, as a 'permanent' employee in an established organization, or run your own business.

The most successful workers today are chameleon-like day-to-day value adders who are flexible and adapt well to changing circumstances: there are temps – the fastest growing category of employees – and there are consultants, people who market themselves instead of relying on temp agencies for work. (But then 'consultant' is just a fancy word for temp.)

Temping is not just for clerical workers anymore, but doctors, lawyers, engineers, bankers, scientists, executives, teachers, salespeople, programmers, librarians, trapeze artists, athletes, singers, and everyone else you can think of. With this development, temps are no longer stigmatized as 'less than employees,' and established companies are even setting up their own internal temp agencies, complete with training centers, to meet their unpredictable staffing needs. And while it is true that established organizations will always have core groups of 'permanent' employees (more than three years), their roles will continue to blur inside and outside of the organizations.

Already, core groupers and temps work side by side as value adders in transitory project teams – teams composed of members who may be in the same building, across the street or around the world linked by technology; teams managed by facilitators instead of bosses; teams that will last just long enough to meet the needs of some customer (the boss, team leader, co-workers, suppliers, clients, consumers, end users) somewhere (in the same building, across the street or around the world).

Of course, many people are choosing to start their own business. Certainly, that option gives you more control over your career, but it will not free you from the need to be a day-to-day value adder: you will need to meet the unpredictable, immediate, short-term demands of a wide range of customers. If you do create your own successful business, you will probably find yourself working as an 'outsource' in the thick of project teams, right alongside temps and core groupers.

What does this mean for you?

Thinking of yourself as the sole proprietor of your skills and abilities is the only way to get in the mood for working in the post-jobs era: everyone is a potential customer. Every unmet need is an opportunity to add value. Every untapped resource is waiting to be mined. If you don't know how to do something, learn. If you don't know how to get the job done, find a way.

To be an effective value adder in the post-jobs era, no matter where you are working, you need to be a multi-skilled rapid learner, who can identify needs quickly, transcend assumptions and regular ways of doing business, and focus on results. Get the job done, whatever the job may be, wherever the job may be, for whomever, whenever, whyever, and however.

Five different ways to add value

Whether you own a business, work as a temp, or work as a 'permanent' employee in an established organization, there are five different ways to add value:

1. Identify a problem that others have not yet identified

Identifying a problem should never sound like criticizing and complaining. Try being a 'cheerful problem spotter' by always proposing at least one solution to every problem you identify.

For example, identify a problem: 'Our customers get very impatient waiting for their orders to be processed. The problem is that people in line are getting mad.'

Propose at least one solution: 'Maybe we should hand out free french fries to customers so they have something to snack on while they are waiting.'

But remember: even if you can't think of a solution, spotting a problem is the first step toward solving it.

Your mantra: spot 'em if you got 'em (cheerfully).

> **❝** I came to this store from another retail operation, which was, frankly, much more successful – higher volume, more activity, better staffed. I immediately saw that I had a lot to contribute. I spent the first few weeks pointing these things out until I realized that everybody was starting to hate me. I realized that I was coming off like a know-it-all and I wasn't even talking about solutions, just problems. I took a step back and went at it with a better attitude. . . . Two years later I am a team leader in that store.
>
> *Department store team leader, formerly team member for two years in the same store, has also worked in two other retail organizations, twenty-six*

2. Solve a problem that others have not yet solved

While the first step to solving a problem is spotting it, the key to solving a problem is how you define it. In the fast-food example above, handing out french fries to the customers waiting in line is a solution to the problem defined this way: 'People in line are getting mad.'

But think about redefining the problem using the word *because*: 'People are getting mad *because* they are waiting too long.' Defined in these terms, the problem that needs solving is cutting down the amount of time they are actually waiting. Once you realize that people are waiting in line too long because it takes too long to fill an order, the solution will be about speeding up the process of filling an order. To arrive at the best solution, you will have to define what is slowing down the process: 'The process takes too long *because* . . .'

> **❝** This may sound stupid, but I think my biggest contribution

so far has been figuring out that the air conditioning wasn't cooling off the building because there were gaps in the windows and doors. It took some effort to fix, but, until I showed up, they couldn't figure out what was wrong. They just knew it was too hot.

Juggling three part-time jobs, waiting tables, supply teaching, and loading boxes onto vans in a warehouse, twenty-four

3. Invent a brand-new service or product

Change creates needs, so new products and services usually grow out of change. Overnight delivery was made necessary because more and more people started doing business regardless of geographical distance and the pace of business interactions accelerated dramatically, creating an increased demand for overnight deliveries. Prozac resulted from a heightened awareness of depression as an illness and advances in pharmaceutical science. There wouldn't be much demand for Web site designers and Internet consultants without the Internet. And so on. Every change happening around you is giving rise to unmet needs – needs that can be met by the creation of a new service or product.

Your mantra: in every change happening around you, look for unmet needs you can meet by inventing a new service or product.

❝ We wanted to publish a journal about solutions that wasn't policy focused but more looking at individuals and groups and what they are actually doing in this growing community service movement. It is not about partisanship or government solving problems, but what can people do at a local level to make our communities more healthful and liveable. We spent the first six months getting organized. We did focus groups that consisted of sitting around on the floor eating bagels, and talking about what the magazine should be. It was kind of a whirlwind of networking and traveling around, making decisions, and low and behold, we had a magazine.

Co-founder of a monthly magazine of volunteerism for people in their twenties, twenty-seven

4. Improve an existing service or product

Even if you can't think of a new service or product, there is always room to improve those which already exist. Just think, no one liked reading faxes when they came on shiny, scrolled-up sheets of paper, but now there are plain paper fax machines. Struggling with carbon paper is no longer necessary now we have photocopiers. McDonald's used to serve burgers in Styrofoam containers, but now they use paper. The list goes on.

Your mantra: make it faster, easier, more efficient, more effective, more attractive, cooler, less expensive, or whatever.

> **❝** I developed my own career opportunity at a paper company. I work with the marketing department to focus on new customers and develop new markets. Usually, printers buy paper directly from paper manufacturers like us and then the printer gets a contract with a company like Coca Cola to print labels for the soda bottles. I thought, 'That's backwards. Why not go to Coke and ask them what printers they do business with and sell Coke on our paper so their printer has to buy the paper from us.' It's a pretty ballsy move, but I saw tons of advantages. The people I work for had no idea how to pursue this, so I treated it as my own little business. I started hanging out in the hallways of all the big beverage companies and asking a lot of questions. As long as I am creating these new opportunities in new markets, the company will let me continue to do my own thing.
>
> *Former unpaid intern at a large accounting/consulting firm,*
> *worked as a manufacturer's representative, salesperson,*
> *and now working for a paper company trying to*
> *develop new market opportunities, twenty-six*

5. Deliver an existing service or product in a timely, competent manner

To be a value adder, you don't have to be the one to identify and solve problems, invent or improve services and products. Someone has to deliver the post every day, dispense the medicine, write the news, lay out the newspaper, print the magazine, operate the television cameras, change the oil, send the faxes, answer the phones, take messages, package the CDs, flip the burgers, and sell the Roller Blades. In other words, someone has got to do the work.

Your mantra: whatever you do, get the job done; do it well; with a big smile on your face; and do it on time. You'll be a gold mine for anyone smart enough to hire you.

> 66 One of my instructors at the university was the Dean and she called me up three days before the semester began and said she had my résumé there. I had applied for a photographer's assistant job, but then their graphic arts instructor got sick, so she called and said, 'I know you don't have experience teaching, but you do have experience in graphic arts, would you be interested in substituting for three weeks?' I did some heavy cramming and my three week substitution went fine. Then the teacher for whom I was substituting got worse, went into the hospital and then passed away, and they asked me to stay for the semester, since I had developed a rapport with the students. Then they asked me to teach for another semester and I really enjoyed it, but it was very technical to teach. But then I also got them to let me teach a computer art class, which I loved.
>
> *Artist, craftsman, former university teacher, computer graphics designer, thirty-one*

The seven-step plan for selling your added value

Once you've identified how to add value, you still have to sell people on what you can bring to the table. The key to being an effective salesperson for your added value is to think of everyone as your customer: your boss, team leader, co-workers, subordinates, suppliers, and vendors (as well as your traditional customers).

Here is a seven-step plan for selling your added value to any decision maker, anytime, anywhere:

1. Define the value for yourself

Until you define for yourself the value you are capable of adding in any situation, it will be impossible to sell that value to anyone else. All you have to do is match your skills and abilities with someone else's needs and wants. Of course, some needs and wants will be sitting there waiting for you when you arrive, like a problem that no one has yet solved; a product that needs to be delivered in a competent, timely manner; or a service that needs improvement.

When a need is sitting there waiting for you, your first key move is to identify that need. Then you will be able to figure out how you can apply your skills and abilities to solve the problem, deliver the product, or improve the service.

However, many needs and wants are dormant – a problem that others have not yet identified, a brand-new service or product not yet invented. Dormant needs remain below the surface until you create them or at least until you make your 'customer' aware of them.

In such a case, the first key move is using your imagination to discover or invent the need. Then, of course, you can figure out how to apply your skills and abilities to define the problem; or create the service or product.

No matter where you are working, no matter what you are doing, there will be tons of unmet needs, waiting to be identified, discovered or invented. Keep a running list of those needs in a notebook. Set aside time once a week to review your running list and brainstorm about ways to match those needs with your skills and abilities.

> **❝** The show is supposed to grab the attention of young people, and they should look to me to say what's hot and what's not. I am their target audience. For example, the opening music – it's okay, but I want them to play the kind

of music that, if you are in the kitchen and you hear the music on the television, you are going to say, 'what's that? what's going in? I want to listen to that.' I have ideas for how they can appeal to people my age. That's what I have to offer along with running errands and making photocopies, you know.

College senior doing a placement at a television station, twenty-two

2. Create an effective sales message to persuade the right decision makers

In order to communicate to others what you have defined for yourself (the value you are capable of adding), you need a sales message.

The key to developing an effective sales message is understanding your audience. You want to aim your message at the right decision makers: people who have the power to buy the value you are selling and make a deal and become paying (money and otherwise) 'customers.'

Once you identify the right decision makers, you need to target your sales message accordingly – and that takes some market research. If you have direct access to your audience (for instance, people you already work with), take some time to ask them a bunch of questions. Find out if they perceive the same need you have identified, discovered, or invented. See if they have already taken any steps to address the need, if they have plans to do so, or if they are open to the idea. Ask how they might envision the project, the time frame, the budget, or staffing. Do these people think your skills and abilities might fit the need? Would they be open to a proposal? What kinds of things would they need to see to take your proposal seriously? In what format? How long? How much detail? When would be a good time to submit a proposal? And so on. If you don't have direct access to your target audience, try to answer these questions for yourself before you develop your sales message.

Gather as much market research as you possibly can from

whatever sources are available to you: consult other people who have some experience with or knowledge of your target audience; read background material, check out their Web site, and so on.

In the end, the most effective sales message will have all of the following characteristics:

> ▷ It will be summed up in one sentence.
> ▷ It will be elaborated upon in the form of a proposal.
> ▷ It will answer the questions who, what, where, why, when, and how.
> ▷ It will play off your audience's beliefs and take them one step further without contradicting their values and assumptions.
> ▷ It will be believable.
> ▷ It will be memorable.

❝ To get the job, first I had to sell them. They said, 'Why should we hire you?' And I basically told them, 'Look, I am awesome at sales, I want to sell for you, and I'll eat what I kill. You know, work on 100% commission.' How could they say no?

Awesome salesperson, twenty-two

3. Deliver the message

To deliver your message, you have to package it: in print, video, audio, electronic, or in person. If you can, make the package reflect the message, like the guy who sent a letter in a Perrier bottle to the CEO of the Perrier company, that said, 'Help, I am a marketing genius trapped in the body of an MBA.' The reason why this packaging reflected the message is because marketing requires creativity and cleverness and this was a very clever package. Sometimes trying to be clever will make you seem like a wise-ass, so it's a bit risky. The more clever you are, the more likely it is that you will be remembered; however, it is even more important to seem professional than it is to seem clever.

The best combination for message delivery is professional, interesting, and useful: a clear concise cover letter that highlights the one-sentence summary of your message along with a brief proposal answering who, what, where, why, when, and how you will add value. If you can, also demonstrate your ability to add value by sending along a free sample.

Once you have packaged your message, make every contact a multiple contact: mail, telephone, fax, overnight, and e-mail every contact. (If you are having a hard time getting through, don't forget to make friends with the gatekeeper, see page 102.) Then, follow up and try to get feedback on your proposal so you can determine whether this decision-maker is a live possibility or a dead end.

> ❝ I showed up in person, waited all day in the waiting area because I didn't have an appointment. The managing editor finally let me come in for an interview at the end of the day. I could tell she hadn't even seen my résumé or any of the writing samples I had sent, but my persistence paid off because I got the job.
> *Former staff writer for several newsstand magazines, working now as a freelance writer, twenty-nine*

4. Close the deal

Once you've got a live possibility, it's like having a fish on the end of a fishing line. All you have to do is real 'em in. There are six steps to closing any deal:

1. Move the conversation to specific terms – time, place, and money.

2. Know in advance your own desired terms (what you will ask for) and your own bottom line (without which you are willing to walk away).

3. Ask your customer right away 'What are your ideal terms?'

4. State your desired terms, stop talking, wait, be patient, and keep waiting until your customer says something –

anything. Maybe he will accept your desired terms, maybe he will say 'No way,' or maybe he will say, 'Maybe.' You won't know unless you listen very carefully.

5. Stop and think about your response. If she says 'Yes,' then you just closed the deal. If she says 'Maybe,' or equivocates in any way return to step 4 – repeat your desired terms, stop, wait, and listen (keep doing this until you get to 'Yes' or 'No way'). If she says 'No way,' go straight to step 6.

6. Ask your customer 'What is your bottom line?' Or, 'What do you need from me to close this deal?' Then, once again, listen carefully. If your customer's bottom line is less than yours, you have nothing to lose because you are prepared to walk away. State your own bottom line and return to step 4 – stop and listen carefully. If your customer's bottom line is more than yours, go ahead and accept your customer's bottom line terms: you just closed the deal.

> ❝ Closing a deal takes patience, above all else. You can't let the silence get to you. The more talking your customer does, the more you learn about what they are willing to accept. You have to ask good questions, but mostly let them talk. If they want to buy and you don't say anything, they will just keep raising the price on themselves until they get to what they are willing to pay.
>
> *Car salesman, also building multilevel marketing business, and working part-time as a sales representative for an advertising specialties company, twenty-eight*

5. Add the value you promised to add and always go the extra mile

Reputation is everything. Never sell something you can't deliver. Once you sell it, you had better deliver it.

Brainstorm all the resources available to you and make a plan.

Start at the end-goal and the deadline and work backward. Set intermediate goals and deadlines along the way to keep you on course and on schedule. Then, schedule daily actions to meet each intermediate goal. Stay in personal contact with the customer, give regular updates on your progress, and always be honest. And always go the extra mile: go one step beyond the specifications; add the bells, whistles, and tie a bow on it; get it done early; and when it comes time to be paid, discount the price.

If you are worried that you will not have the time, resources, or ability to go the extra mile, do this: at the outset, understate whatever you know you can achieve, then achieve what you know you can and you will be going the extra mile. Give yourself more time than you know you will need, then finish the job in the time you need and you will be going the extra mile. Overstate your price by 20 percent and then offer a 20 percent discount. Promising less with the intention of delivering more is also a good insurance policy just in case you run into cost overruns, delays, or other complications.

> 66 It's simple, I just never promise more than I can deliver and then I kill myself to deliver more.
> *Sales representative for a consumer products company,*
> *twenty-three*

6. Get paid

When you close a deal, commit the terms to paper, initial it, and pass it along to your 'customer' for his or her initials. Do this even if you are working on a specific project with a co-worker or your boss or your best friend.

Simply write a memo saying, 'My understanding is that we agreed that we will work together on ____. You would do ___, Sam would do ____, and I would do ____, by next Thursday. Is this your understanding too?'

This kind of committing to paper need not necessarily be a legally binding contract, but is meant to confirm that everybody knows what is expected of one another. Confirming everybody's understanding at the outset of each project will substantially reduce the chances of misunderstanding and conflict as you work together.

If you are in business for yourself, or working as a consultant (temp) on a project, then there are very important legal reasons for committing agreements to paper. From a legal standpoint, committing terms to paper and having both parties sign the paper is proof that you have made an enforceable agreement, otherwise known as a contract. In order to have an enforceable contract, you need to include the following details:

> ▷ What are you promising to do?
> ▷ What is the other person promising to do?
> ▷ For each: When? and Where? (And sometimes Why? and How?)

Believe it or not, that's all you need to make a contract enforceable. Of course, many contracts include a lot of other terms, but those stated above are the only ones you need.

Of course you want to be fairly remunerated for the value you add, but remember, there is always more than money at the bottom line if you look hard enough. Especially if you are working as a 'permanent' employee in an established company, don't be satisfied with money, health insurance, and contributions to your pension plan. In addition, go after these nonfinancial self-building rewards:

> ▷ New marketable skills
> ▷ Relationships with people who can help you
> ▷ The tangible results of your hard work – proof of your ability to add value
> ▷ Greater responsibility and increased creative freedom
> ▷ More power to plan your own schedule

❝ Some people will definitely try to stiff you. There is no

question about it. They figure, 'You are in business for yourself. You're just starting out. What are you going to do about it?' You've got to get a contract. Even then, a lot of times it's not worth it to go to court to enforce it.

Former information systems consultant at a large consulting firm, now a sole proprietor selling computer programming and graphics, systems design, and some Web design services, twenty-five

7. Provide follow-up service

Follow-up service will do two things: (1) it will help you build an ongoing relationship with your customers; and (2) it will provide a quality check on whatever you are selling. Follow-up service will also help you win repeat business, referral business, and word of mouth, as well as testimonials and letters of reference.

What do I mean by follow-up service? Call your customers when the project is all done and do a quality check – solicit their feedback: 'Were you satisfied with the results? Was the project completed on time? Were you satisfied with how you were treated? Were your expectations met? Were your expectations exceeded? Did you think the price was fair? What could I have done to serve you better? What was the best thing about our working together?'

If you did a great job, these questions will remind your customer of what a great job you did and reinforce the positive impression you have made. On top of that, your customers will be very impressed that you are taking the time to solicit their feedback and make sure they were satisfied. If they were supersatisfied, they will tell you and you will know who to go to for references in the future, as well as repeat business, and introductions to other potential customers. Maybe one of your most satisfied customers will become your greatest mentor.

On the other hand, if you find out from your quality check that your customer was not satisfied, do whatever you have to do to make it right: offer to correct any mistakes or improve the results for free; refund their money; offer to make adjustments for free, even if it's because they changed their minds after you were done. Just leave them happy, if you possibly can. Whether you get positive or negative feedback from your quality check, the most important thing is to use whatever feedback you do get to improve your performance in the future.

> 66 We always call to get feedback from our customers at the end of a project. And my boss will sometimes have to go back and change certain things for free, but she'll do it no matter what it is – which is a pain, but it's just a great lesson and one that I am definitely trying to apply in my own work. For example, when I do work for my boss, I seek feedback and try to express the same willingness to correct mistakes with a giant smile on my face, if you know what I mean.
>
> *Administrative assistant at a mid-size consulting firm,*
> *twenty-two*

Ten opportunities to be a day-to-day value adder

Once you start looking, you will run across new opportunities to add value with every step you take. If you are keeping a running list of value-adding opportunities, you will soon have a whole lot more opportunities than you can possibly handle. While you juggle as many possibilities as you can, you also need to be making strategic decisions about which opportunities to put on the back burner and which ones to focus on.

You can't sell ten proposals at once. On the other hand, in an uncertain world, it is very important to diversify: try to balance at least two different projects at any given time.

The following are ten opportunities to be a day-to-day value adder:

1. Just a 'job'-ing

When you are not learning, building relationships, and tackling creative challenges in your 'job,' what are you doing there? You are probably working there just to pay the bills. That's when the job starts to feel like 'just a job.' Most people think that the only jobs which feel like 'just a job' are low-level, go-nowhere jobs – what some people refer to as McJobs.

Of course, everything is relative. No job is just a job, unless you decide it's going to be. *Don't make this mistake.* Time is too precious and you have none of it to waste. Whether you are working one hour, forty hours, or one hundred hours a week, no matter what you are doing, you owe it to yourself to make the most of every single minute.

If you are not learning, building relationships, and tackling creative challenges in your 'just a job,' then you already have a tremendous creative challenge staring you right in the face: how can you transform your time at work into a fulfilling, self-building opportunity? Study your time there. Exactly what do you do? Keep a notebook for a week and write down everything you do and what time you do it. Then brainstorm ideas about how you can maximize the potential of your situation and use it to add value to yourself. Once you see your job as more than 'just a job,' you can be a day-to-day value adder in absolutely any workplace.

> 66 As funny as this sounds, I feel I learned more 'skills' in my bartender training than any other job I have held. My training focused on developing 'regular' customers which taught me some excellent listening and memory skills as well as sharpening my interpersonal skills in dealing with a wide range of personalities. I use these skills every day in my personal and professional life as they are applicable to just about any situation.
> *Former physical education teacher, personal trainer, bartender, currently working as a sales representative, thirty*

2. Fast-tracking

Just like they track kids in school, organizations track employees at work. Fast-track positions are intended to move the best educated, most skilled, capable, ambitious, and hard working employees into leadership positions as quickly as possible. Most organizations have fast tracks, either officially or *de facto*.

If you are in the fast track in any organization, you will have access to amazing resources. The organization will pay for outside training courses, inside training materials, and may even pay for you to get an advanced degree. You will get to spend time with all the big shots; the senior executives will take you out to lunch; they will probably introduce you to clients and let you sit in on important meetings. You will also get the best assignments, while others are slaving away up to their ears in grunt work; you may get to travel to interesting places; you might even get to put your name on some high-profile products.

If you are in a fast track, recognize it and play it for all it's worth: suck up every available resource as if you are strip-mining the organization. Learn as if there's no tomorrow. Make yourself invaluable to every big shot you can get your hands on. Throw yourself into every project, don't be afraid to take chances, go ahead and make mistakes, push yourself to innovate, and ask if you can put your name on it when your done. Stay until you've stripped the mine bare. But remember, fast-trackers also work the longest, hardest hours – the moment you feel yourself burning out, use that fast-track position as a stepping stone to a new opportunity.

    " During the recruiting process, I was able to meet most of the people that I would end up working with. The training has been incredible; they are investing more and more in the training. The opportunity to gain skills there was amazing and there is a lot of mentoring. I feel like I have had the chance to do some amazing things: To travel, to have enormous responsibility, but also the support necessary to do the job. They keep pushing and, so far, I am just riding this job like a roller coaster.

Fast-tracker at a big six accounting/consulting firm,
twenty-five

3. Reinvent your role in any organization

As long as you want to keep working in any one organization, be prepared to reinvent yourself and your role in that organization over and over again.

Preparing to reinvent yourself means you have to diversify within the organization:

> ▷ Look for multiple customers – do not be content to work for one boss.
> ▷ Juggle multiple responsibilities – do not settle for a narrow set of tasks.
> ▷ Work in several skill areas – do not let yourself be pigeonholed.
> ▷ Be on friendly terms with lots of people – do not be part of a clique.
> ▷ Work on several projects at once – do not let yourself be typecast.

Reinventing yourself over and over again means you have to be like a chameleon:

> ▷ Be comfortable with organizational change.
> ▷ Embrace new rules, new practices, and new people.
> ▷ Be willing to work with one project team today and another one tomorrow.
> ▷ Be content to drop all of your current responsibilities and tasks and assume a whole bunch of new ones.
> ▷ Welcome the chance to work in a new office, new city, new region, or a new country. If you don't want to be an organizational nomad, you must learn to be a corporate chameleon.

But don't wait for organizational change to reinvent your role. Keep a regular inventory of work that needs to be done and work you would like to be involved in. When one project is running out, create detailed proposals for several new projects you would like to work on, and keep submitting them until you get a new assignment. Remember, when submitting proposals, always keep an open mind. Even if your proposal is not accepted, it may inspire a whole new project, or at least give your boss the idea of staffing you on a project related to your proposal.

> **❝** I started there as a clerical temp and one of the things I was asked to do was type up a posting for a job as a copywriter in the direct marketing department. I typed it up and attached a note saying why I thought I would be a great person for that job. I worked for three years writing copy for direct mail. Then they started shopping out most of the direct marketing to an outside company, which eliminated the need for most of the department. I knew that they were developing some new services and I asked around quite a bit to see if there was a role for me on one of the new services. For a while I worked as a customer service rep on the travel service. But when my boss started rejecting all the copy being done for the travel service by this direct marketing company, of course I offered to do it. Now, all the copy for the travel service is done in-house, by me.
>
> *Working in a major credit card company, first as a temp, then in direct marketing, then in the travel services, twenty-seven*

4. Leaving without really leaving

It costs a lot of money to recruit and train a new employee. New employees need time to get acclimated to an organization's corporate culture; get to know the other employees, not to mention managers, suppliers, and customers; learn how things are done in the organization; develop the right skills; and gain sufficient experience. It can take three, six, twelve, or eighteen months before a new employee adds more value than he or she costs an organization.

If you leave after a short time, the organization is not going to get a very good return on the recruiting and training investment they have made in you. Of course, that's their problem. However, their problem may be your opportunity. Why can't you leave your position as a full-time employee, but still add value as a part-time employee, flexitimer, telecommuter, periodic temp, or consultant? You still know your way around, right? You know the people in the organization. You know how they like things done. You have all these valuable skills they've taught you. You still know how to achieve your tasks and meet your responsibilities. Maybe you have a special rapport with certain clients or customers.

Even if they can't have all of you, why shouldn't they keep as much as you are willing to let them? They've already made the investment. From your standpoint, maybe you don't want to work like a dog, but you might value the option to make a little money at your old job, whenever you feel like it. If you are starting your own business, or going back to school, or moving, that option might just keep you afloat during hard times. And don't forget, if you are looking for a new 'permanent' position, most prospective employers will ask you, 'What are you doing right now?' It might be nice to be able to say, 'Well, my former employer just couldn't do without me, so I'm still doing some work for them . . . you know, as a consultant.'

> 66 I made a decision to leave my very first job out of college only five months after starting. Though my departure disappointed a few of the staff members, I maintained a professional and cordial relationship with all of them. I continued to do freelance work for the newspaper. As I furthered my career I was always looking for new opportunities to grow professionally. I was hired [to do] public relations for a motor sports facility, which never had such a position.
>
> *Former assistant to editor of motor sports publication, racing driver, currently director of public relations for a world class motor sports facility, thirty*

5. Effective job juggling

Maybe you are juggling several part-time, low-paying jobs just to pay the bills. Or maybe you are juggling some decent-paying jobs that you hate, just to support a project that you love. Or maybe you are trying to pay for school, or support a placement that's a great learning experience or a great stepping stone. Maybe you're trying to launch a new business. Whatever your reasons, if you are trying to juggle multiple jobs all at once, you run the risk of undermining your effectiveness in one or all of them.

To avoid that result, find synergies between and among your different jobs and use your time, labor, and creativity in each job to add more value in each other. Perhaps the people you work with in one job would like to do business with the people you work with in one of your other jobs, or at least they might like to meet one another.

Think about whether the skills you are learning in one job can be used in one of your other jobs. Maybe there is some overlap among the various projects you are working on in your different jobs. If you are juggling jobs to support a business start-up or another project that you love, you can probably find valuable resources in the workplace that will add value to your business or project – such as using sophisticated computers and other equipment, research materials, expert advice, or help and support from co-workers. Every little bit helps.

> 66 When I was in film school, I also went to work at a big law firm as a night-time legal assistant. My hours were from 11 p.m. to 7 a.m. and then I would go to school during the day. There was all this computer equipment and it was my introduction to being on-line, with Lexus Nexus. So I started to get an education in some of that and it was a tremendous resource. But perhaps the greatest resource there that I was interested in was the other night-time legal assistants who were all in the arts. There was a paralegal who was in *Phantom of the Opera* at the same time she was working at the law firm. There were people

who were actors. You found out about productions that were being planned. For the film I was doing, I used an actress from the law firm, and a composer. At one point in my second year film. I needed a bunch of extras and they all showed up. I also had a lot of production assistants from the law firm who wanted to help out and be involved. It was a great support system.

Film maker, ice skating teacher, used to work as a paralegal,
also teaching college film course, thirty-one

If you are juggling jobs to support your education, you can probably design a research project in school that will be valuable to one of your employers; or take a project from one of your jobs and turn it into a research paper for course credit at school. In order to juggle, you have to make all the balls work together – otherwise you'll keep dropping them.

❝ I wanted to write and teach but I have always had second and third jobs to make money. While I was teaching and doing grant writing at this clinic for pregnant women, I was also doing some editing work on a book project. I was also working at other clinics on a per diem basis. When I got a job at Dana Farber Cancer Institute, doing lab administration, I never actually left the other clinics. Later I was an administrative assistant with an architecture firm that builds hospitals and I thought, 'Great, they can help me get a job in a hospital eventually.' I decided to apply to nursing school and one of the architects where I was working wrote a couple of letters of recommendation for me. I continued working at the women's health clinic probably thirty hours a week while I was in nursing school. Then I started tutoring other nursing students in my program, which gave me a chance to teach and stay on my toes with the material. I still am tutoring a total of about twenty students in all four levels of nursing at any given time. I finished nursing school and now I am at Mass General doing clinical research, which is an unusual role for nurses. During this whole time, I've still had my quilting business, which I do for extra money.

Teacher, writer, quilter, nurse, thirty

6. Job-hopping

Employment relationships are increasingly short-term. Workers will come together in short-term project teams to meet the immediate needs of erratic markets. That means the distinction among permanent workers, temps, and consultants will keep dissolving. If you are job-hopping every year or so, you are living this trend – that's true whether you are hopping voluntarily or because your employer decides that your services are no longer needed.

If you are going to hop, though, make sure to do so gracefully. Here are some job-hopping issues you need to keep in mind:

1. *Benefits:* Learn about the benefits system in the organization where you are working and in the organization to which you may move. Find out when your pension rights vest (if they are only weeks or months away from vesting, maybe you should wait). See if your pension funds are portable or can be cashed out, without penalty. If not, you can probably leave your pension funds in the organization, even if you are no longer an employee, until they become portable or liquid without penalty.

2. *Training:* No matter what you do, never hop until your initial period of intensive training is complete. Never waste an opportunity to acquire marketable skills.

3. *Individuals (future customers):* Even if you leave the organization, try to leave on great terms with as many individuals as possible. Select some decision makers, maybe those you've cultivated during your time in the organization, and make a concerted effort to make them understand your reasons for leaving. Volunteer to finish the projects you are working on, to stay until they find a replacement, and offer to train your replacement. Remember, the individuals with whom you build relationships are going to be future customers of your added value, or mentors, or maybe even your friends.

4. *Offer to leave without leaving:* If you hop through enough

jobs, leaving without leaving, you might build a pretty impressive client list, and before you know it, you'll have created your own consulting business.

❝ I left the firm where I first worked because the development process for young attorneys was not adequate. I went to work for a smaller, not as well known firm. I knew I was giving up a lot of money, but I also knew I would be much more marketable. Because I would have a lot more hands-on experience and a lot more responsibility and a lot more training. When the firm had some internal troubles, I figured, 'If I don't move on now, there may be a negative connotation being with a firm which is falling apart.' So I decided to leverage my new skills and experience sooner rather than later. I went to a large international firm which is like a megafirm, the kind that does huge corporate transactions and I am adding that to my repertoire now.

Lawyer, twenty-eight

7. Entrepreneuring

Remember that the main reason why so many people under the age of thirty-four are actively trying to start their own businesses today is that the three traditional obstacles for young entrepreneurs have all but disappeared. (1) It costs much less money to start a business today than before because most new businesses start up in the service sector (many in information and technology) and require little space and equipment. (2) Since everyone has to keep learning new skills, knowledge, and practices, the learning curve has leveled out considerably for workers at all levels of experience – especially in start-ups driven by innovation. (3) Risking job security to start your own business is not such a big risk in the post-jobs era.

If you want to be an entrepreneur, you can go right ahead and buy a store or something, but your best bet will be to follow the three trends making it possible for you to start a business in the first place.

1. Try to start a business that requires very little investment and, if at all possible, no debt. That means you might have to start slowly, maybe even while you still have a 'day job.' As you begin to generate revenue, grow the business with the money that's coming in and keep feeding yourself (and maybe your business) with your day job until you are really up and running. Any business which relies primarily on your time, labor and creativity (service) will have minimal start-up costs.

> **❝** We were going to contract with various restaurants that don't deliver and offer to deliver their food. The only start up costs are stuff people already have and radios and printing – you have to print up the menus. You go in and say I want to start a delivery business. You can either get a flat fee or a discount and you charge the people. I was going to put a couple of twists on it – take the drink orders and then transfer them, deliver beer and wine also – you basically have to deliver for the liquor store and they are paying you a percentage as their delivery person.
> *Retired US Navy flight navigator, in the process of starting up a service business, twenty-nine*

2. Try starting a business in an emerging field (like Web design) or a business which flows from a great idea, so you don't have to compete with established business people who already have more skills, knowledge, and experience, over and above their existing customer base and cash flow.

> **❝** About three years ago, we were having a party and this guy Craig was there getting people interested in this quirky game that no one else at the party had ever heard of. He claimed to have the ability to link movie actor Kevin Bacon to any and every actor/ actress who had appeared in movies or television after 1950. I remember thinking, 'Why Kevin Bacon?' Then he gave us a demonstration: 'Warren Beatty – Warren Beatty was in *Dick Tracy* with Dustin Hoffman who was in *Rainman* with Tom Cruise who was in *A Few Good Men* with Kevin Bacon.' Immediately, people began barking out the most obscure actors and actresses but no one could stump Craig. Later, I found out that Craig

and three of his fraternity brothers were being featured on radio stations, television shows and in newspapers all across the country. They have even published a book about their game, which is called 'The Six Degrees of Kevin Bacon.' I guess they are the undisputed 'industry leaders' and the only ones in the industry.

Administrative director of a strategic think tank, twenty-three.

3. Instead of looking at leaving your day job as a detriment (giving up a steady income or whatever), leverage your former experience in an established company to give you more credibility with your would-be customers. Also, get all the help you can get from the individuals with whom you built relationships during your time in the organization. And, consider trying to sell them your new service.

❝ When they ask what I've done before, I tell them the name of the law firm where I used to work and I tell them that firm was my first client in my new business, which is true.

Formerly a practicing attorney, now running a travel agency
catering to lawyers, thirty-four

8. Knowledge working

In the post-information revolution economy, the information industry is giving birth to the knowledge and meaning industries. (Meaning is knowledge plus interpretation.) But it's hard for any one individual to acquire expertise in more than one or two fields, and it's impossible to acquire as much expertise as you can use in your life and career.

On the other hand, it is very efficient for individuals to divide up all the hard work of learning, divide up the acquisition of expertise, and purchase the expertise from each other as needed. Of course, people with unique knowledge have always found markets to sell what they know. Monopolizing a particular field of knowledge and finding markets to sell that knowledge is the cornerstone of all the traditional professions (law, medicine, engineering, architecture, academia).

The reason why the category 'professional' is now applied to virtually every non-manual-labor job is that virtually all work today requires the manipulation of unique knowledge. Today, the acquisition of expertise in virtually any field will make you a meaning-industry 'professional,' otherwise known as an 'expert.' Once you are an 'expert' in any field, you just have to package (in print, video, audio, digital, or in person) and then sell your expertise.

> 66 The only reason you could call me a Web expert is because most people know next to nothing about the Web. People like me have spent a lot of time thinking and learning about it, frankly just playing a lot of the time. I can find my way around, design your Web page better than most people could. So all of a sudden, I'm a consultant.
>
> *College junior, twenty*

9. Volunteering for community service

Bring your skills and abilities to bear on a need you perceive in your community. In just a few hours a week you can add so much value and improve the quality of life for yourself, your family, and your neighbors. On top of that, you're bound to meet people, learn skills, collect evidence of your ability to add value, and probably even have some fun. Working together on a community service project is a wonderful way to spend time with your family, or old friends, or the brand-new friends you will make in the process. Volunteering to work for a charitable organization, or a cause you believe in, is also a fabulous way to learn. Since you are volunteering your time, people will be thrilled to take the time to teach you some very valuable skills, such as fundraising, public relations, event planning, and more.

If you really put some time into a particular charity or cause, you may find yourself moving quickly into a leadership position, which is a great way to learn some leadership and management skills. It's a whole lot easier to become the leader of a volunteer organization than an organization run by paid staff. Usually, whoever puts in the most time becomes a leader in a pretty short period of time. A lot of people don't

May the Internet be with you

Take advantage of all the resources available on the Internet: (1) You can check classified ads all over the country, provided the community in which you are looking has a local newspaper which is on-line. (2) There are also numerous Web-based services designed to offer a range of career advice, as well as specific job postings. Some will help you submit job applications by e-mail. (3) Of course, if you are interested in researching a particular industry, you can find a lot of useful information (and specific opportunities) via industry related Web sites and usenet groups. Such groups may be sponsored by a trade or professional association, a particular company or organization, or by interested individuals like yourself. (4) You can also use key-word searches to generate lists of potential employers in various fields and industries. (5) You can gather tons of information about a company or organization by visiting their Web site. Often companies and organizations will post a list of specific job openings for which they are seeking applicants. (6) Finally, consider inviting potential employers to visit your own Web site to find concrete proof of your ability to add value. Don't just post a nice picture of yourself and your résumé. Rather, get together as many examples of your previous work as you possibly can and post them on your Web site, allowing potential employers to click on and take a look at what you've done before. Also, provide links to individuals who will give you raving recommendations if they are contacted by a potential employer.

want the responsibilities of leadership, which is why there is so much more room at the top than there is in the middle or at the bottom of any organization.

❝ I got interested in Habitat for Humanity. It interested me because it was people volunteering and actually building something. I took a leadership role for that short project, leading the roofing team and the framing team. I put in about a week, about forty hours. Then I got involved in a project where I got to go to schools and teach architecture in an elementary school in West Philadelphia, a pretty desolate area. I was paired up with an architect. We taught this kindergarten class one day a week for half a year. We would take them out of the classrooms and into the neighborhoods and talk about structures in their neighborhood. We would also show them structures from the larger world. In the end, they created an African village, building small structures, and they learned about how to create a community. You would think it would be over the head of a kindergarten kid, but it wasn't.

Working as a project architect/intern in an architecture firm, in preparation for taking the architecture exam, twenty-four

10. Nest feathering

No matter where else in the world you are adding value, make sure you have time and energy to add value in your personal life. Feather your own nest. Work on home renovation projects. Mop the floor. Build a bookshelf. Change the oil in your car. Seal the driveway. Manage your financial investments. Collect pennies. Build your body with exercise, healthy food, and plenty of rest. Meditate. Pray. Read books. Study. Practice a new skill. Teach your children or your nieces or nephews or siblings or cousins. Connect with your friends. Have a deep sharing talk with your spouse or your lover. Or a quiet loving nap. Or make love.

❝ The most important thing to me is my own quality of life, my home life. How comfortable is my family? Do I have enough time to spend with them? Are we happy and healthy? If all that is not in order, then nothing else even matters. So, I feel like my first responsibility is tending to things at home.

Former investment banker, taking some time off, thirty-one

As you maximize every opportunity to add value, keep building yourself from within: accumulate marketable skills, build relationships with people who can help you, and collect proof of your ability to add value in any workplace. Remain flexible and always be ready to adapt to each new experience. As you do, continue picking up the bits and pieces of your success everywhere you go and in everything you do.

Moving your life toward balance

In a profoundly insecure world, we owe it to ourselves to be our own greatest sources of security. We can no longer anchor ourselves to society's old-fashioned institutions (the corporation, government, schools, associations, or even the traditional family). We must create our own centers of gravity and anchor ourselves from within. That requires a great deal of balance.

> **"** I didn't like the lifestyle we were leading because my husband had a terrible commute. I never got to see him because when he came home I had to go to work in the dorm. I never got to see my friends, and I only had one weekend off a month. So I quit my job and we moved to New Jersey where my husband had a job offer. In the same month, we were trying to move and I was trying to figure out what I was going to do. So we just left for three weeks and biked around Alaska. It was awesome, we saw mountains and glaciers and whales and got into good shape.
>
> *Scientist, high school chemistry teacher, now attending graduate school to gain teaching certification, twenty-eight*

> **"** The people who are married or have kids just can't compete if they want to spend any time with their family. They all just seem to have given up hope on having a personal life. That's why I just don't think I can last here. I'm not going to live like that.
>
> *Junior-level consultant in first year in a big six accounting/consulting firm, twenty-five*

> **"** At one time we went down to an emergency assistance unit for about four days and then they placed us in a homeless shelter, a homeless hotel. This was like a very spiritual time for us, because all we had was our hearts and our goals, beliefs and ambitions. My girlfriend had two kids already, they were nine and eight and they were with us all the time. We were in this shelter for about eleven months. It was roach ridden, and there were a lot of real down-and-outs. We are now in a three-bedroom apartment in New York and we got married last December; we have a nine-month-old son and my mother now lives

with us. We feel very lucky. Nothing is wasted, every life experience serves you at every level.

Formerly homeless and receiving welfare, worked for a while as a Wendy Burger's assistant manager, now working in a bookstore, selling phone services through a multilevel marketing company, and creating his own system for teaching chess, thirty-two

❝ My parents both worked so much when I was a kid and they made a lot of money. They still do and that's great. But, there's no way I am doing that. When I was nine, it was like they were divorced. They took turns being at home and being part of the family. I practically never saw them in the same room at the same time.

Second-year college student, nineteen

❝ I convinced myself that I wasn't enjoying myself and decided to quit my job. I just kind of thought I needed to do something else. Unfortunately, I had no idea what I wanted that to be. What it ended up being was a one-year stay on Hilton Head Island. It was really supposed to be a time for me to get away and try to figure out what I was going to do with the rest of my life.

Former computer programmer, golf course maintenance worker, computer software trainer, now working as chief financial officer of a small consulting firm, twenty-eight

❝ Four things are very important to me: my fiancé, my family and friends, work and golf. It's pretty hard to find time for all of these all of the time. But I fortunately have a very understanding fiancé and boss (not the same person; at least most of the time).

Engineer, formerly engineering assistant, also a former tennis instructor, twenty-five

❝ When I was 18, I worked at a coffee shop in a mall in Portland. I was living with my parents, working full-time, and saving up about $4,000 for a trip. Then I went away for four months, to the Netherlands, Belgium, Brussels, France, Spain, Portugal and I spent a month in Ireland. When I got back and moved out of my parents' house, I worked for a natural food store in Portland. I spent time in

Idaho and Utah and did the whole canyon lands and did the Tetons and the San Juan Islands. But, mostly I was saving to travel more later. I flew to Amsterdam and spent some time traveling from Holland to France to Switzerland and then I spent some time in Italy and then took a boat to Greece. I also traveled in Africa. . . . We all had our excuses for being there. I was there and I am awfully poor. I don't know how I was affording it, but I was.

Traveler, formerly juggling numerous retail service jobs, now studying photography, twenty-four

Moving your life toward balance

There is so much pressure on the individual in today's world that keeping our lives in balance is not so easy. The most ambitious people of our generation look around and see themselves starting careers in a fiercely competitive economy with more and more people fighting over smaller and smaller pieces of the pie. That's why so many people become workaholics, working sixty, seventy, eighty hours a week, sacrificing everything for achievement, including time with family and friends, their personal well-being, and sometimes even their ethics.

Others of our generation are dropping out of the rat race altogether. Some call them 'slackers' – I prefer to call them 'lifaholics.' Most of these people have decided that trying to shape a stellar career in today's economy is just not worth it. So they work primarily to pay the bills, seeking success and security and cultivating their creativity outside the realm of a career, investing time in relationships with the people they care about, caring for their personal well-being; and staying close to their moral center.

The lifaholics and workaholics of our generation have two things in common. First, both seem to live according to an 'all-or-nothing' philosophy: workaholics fear that if they don't give their all – if they relax for even a moment – they may lose the race and get nothing for all their hard work.

Lifaholics fear that if they invest any part of their self-esteem in their careers – if they seek even a sliver of their success, security, creative fulfillment, and well-being through work – they will somehow be sucked into the ethos and values of the rat race (or worse, the rat race itself) and never escape.

What is second thing that lifaholics and workaholics have in common? They are frequently the very same people.

While workaholics seem to look upon lifaholics with bemusement, most secretly envy their carefree ways. When workaholics burn out from the excesses of competition and achievement, they often go through periods of lifaholism, which can last weeks or months or years. These binges on life sometimes involve travel to far away exotic locations. Sometimes, they involve travel no further than to their old bedroom in their parents' home.

In some cases, parenthood or other family matters are involved. There may be a creative endeavor brewing – writing, painting, singing, dancing, photography, cooking, film, comedy, circuit design, athletic training, or brewing. Maybe there is an entrepreneurial project at the end of the tunnel. Sometimes it's a return to student life and an advanced degree. Sooner or later, they feel rested and recharged, or they've had a chance to express their creativity in new ways, or they are simply bored and chomping at the bit to get back into the rat race. And then, they jump right back in, at full speed, and it's as if they never even left.

The constant tension between workaholism and lifaholism depends upon an obsolete split between the workplace and the home; the public and the private; the economic and the personal. As the boundaries traditionally demarcating work dissolve before our eyes, these old-fashioned distinctions no longer hold up. Almost nobody works nine to five anymore. Workers today are perpetually on call. Most people take sick days now to get some rest, relieve stress, attend to personal needs, or handle family issues. If they have no sick days left, some people have to bring their kids to work. Many people have home offices. Everybody takes at least some work home with them.

Meanwhile, most established organizations are wising up, instituting flexitime, part-time, compressed time, job sharing, and sabbaticals; replacing sick days with wellness days; setting up daycare centers; supporting telecommuting (flexi-place) and underwriting home office expenses. There is a new merger frenzy: merging the workplace and the home; the public and private; the economic and personal.

With no clear boundaries between work and life, it is much harder than it once was to support two separate identities: your 'work self' anchored to the office and your 'life self' anchored to your home and family. That's why so many people become workaholics or lifaholics – at least for as long as they can stand it. Of course, neither choice is feasible, and neither alternative is sustainable. That's why workaholics and lifaholics get sick of their lives and so often switch places.

Avoid this dilemma in your own life. Unite your 'work self' and your 'life self.' Remember, your work and life have always had an obvious common denominator: *you*. Once you are anchored to your own balanced center, you won't have to choose work over life or life over work ever again because your work and life will fit together naturally.

I'll bet you're already moving steadily to anchor yourself to a balanced center. Maybe you're already more firmly anchored than you once were. If so, you are probably stronger, more effective, and more powerful; you probably bounce back more easily from defeat; you probably experience life more fully, enjoy more intense happiness, and savor more sumptuous pleasures.

If you are like most of the people I have interviewed, you are also realizing that it's impossible to actually arrive at a balanced center – the best you can do is keep moving steadily in that direction, guided by clear values and priorities.

▮ Six values and priorities to guide you

To keep yourself moving toward greater balance, it is really important to stay in touch with your deepest values and priorities. You may think of your values and priorities in very unique ways. You probably articulate them much more eloquently than I can. Still, I hope you will consider the following six values and priorities that seem to be transcendent and powerful guides for so many of the people I've interviewed.

1. Quality

You are what you write, say, create, and do (in no particular order). No matter how grand your intentions or how generous and kind you may be as a person, others will know you by your words, actions, and creations. So, always hold yourself to a high standard. Think before you speak. Outline before you write (and always do second drafts). Plan before you act. Double- and triple-check before you finalize your creations. And then go for it.

Don't let yourself be paralyzed by the myth of 100 percent. You see, most people can effectively accomplish 98 percent of the results of almost any undertaking in a very rapid and efficient manner. If you ask me, 98 percent is the highest standard of quality attainable by human beings. I'm not saying that avoidable errors should be excused, but 98 percent does not excuse the kind of errors you can catch on double- and triple-checks. The 2 percent I am talking about is the central character in the myth put about by the procrastinators and failurephobes of the world (the myth is that they get nothing done because they are actually perfectionists). That 2 percent is so relative, so open to debate, so intangible, that it's just not worth agonizing over for even five minutes. So, hold yourself to the highest standard attainable (98 percent) and go for it: speak, write, create, and do.

❝ I take just enough time to do a good job, but I don't take my time, if you know what I mean. There are a lot of people here who are all talk, but they don't get anything done. I've never had complaints about the quality of my work, except from the do-nothings who can't stand to see someone make them look bad.

Former communications department employee in the corporate office of a major consumer products company, now working in the claims investigation department of a large insurance company, twenty-five

2. Integrity

If your boss (or customer) of the day wants you to lie, cheat, steal, or harm others, don't do it. Quit if necessary. Blow the whistle if you think it's appropriate. No matter what, don't get involved in unethical dealings. It's not worth any price. Be honest and honest people will gravitate toward you.

But, let's face it, that's the easy part. I mean, how much judgment or effort is really required to reject downright dishonesty and corruption? The hard part is when integrity requires more than sitting on a high horse in judgment of others. Real integrity requires proactive behavior: breaking your back to deliver, if necessary, when people are counting on you; helping others, even when nobody is there to give you credit; intervening when others are being treated unfairly; and speaking out loud for unpopular causes (if you believe in them).

❝ There has been a growing grass-roots union move- ment among graduate students, and last year it came to a head with a grade strike – where grad student teachers withheld their grades at the end of the semester in a demand for recognition of our teachers' union. I believe that workers should have more power in shaping their own workplaces so I had always been a rank and file member, but now I was asked to step up and be an organizer in my department. It seemed like a big distraction from my academic work. It was a very controversial issue on campus, and learning to organize and persuade people was a huge personal challenge, especially during this strike situation, but ultimately I couldn't say, 'No thanks, I won't be standing up for what I believe in, it's just too inconvenient.' But it turned out to be one of the greatest experiences of my career. Volunteering in the union was a way of being much more engaged in my workplace – I've definitely developed new skills in organizing and administering people and resources. I've gotten to know many of the left-leading academics all over the country who have been involved in the graduate student unionization movement, and I found a community of amazing friends here at home. I know this sounds corny, but I feel like I have stood up for what I believe in, that I've really made an honorable effort to shape the University – my own workplace – and that I've helped shape my profession during a period of profound change.

Former administrative assistant, now a Ph.D. candidate and
labor organizer in graduate student employees union,
twenty-eight

Sometimes the hardest part of integrity is being true to your own identity. While our generation (the first to grow up after affirmative action) makes up the most diverse workforce in history, it remains especially challenging in today's workplace to be a woman, a person of color, gay or lesbian, elderly, especially youthful, or a person with disabilities. Even in today's climate of increasing diversity, there are still so many instances of sexism, racism, homophobia, ageism, and so on. Many are forced to decide every day whether or not to confront the numerous forms of subtle discrimination to which they are subjected. Whether or not to confront subtle sexism or racism is a difficult issue of integrity. What would you decide?

❝ Nobody here needed to know that I am gay. That could have been my little secret like it was when I was younger. Like, not talking about my vacation plans. Not being able to invite people over to my apartment because I live with a man and we share a bedroom. Not being able to keep a picture of my partner on my desk. What it comes down to is not being myself. I'm not going to live like that anymore.

Accountant, twenty-seven

3. Fulfillment

You have every right to expect that living your life will fulfill your deepest aspirations and your fondest hopes. It is true that the majority are so concerned about survival that they do not have the luxury of seeking contentment, actualization, and bliss. But what if you do have that luxury? Those of us who do live comfortably owe it to ourselves to disrupt our comfort in order to reach for the stars. Reaching for the stars does not mean making millions, or winning the Nobel Prize, or being a movie star . . . at least, not necessarily. It means chasing your dreams, whatever they may be, with all of your heart and soul, and keeping up the chase until you catch them.

> ❝ I never woke up in the morning with a burning vision before me proclaiming: 'Anthropology, young man, Anthropology!' This kind of fairy tale vision of your vocation, might be just a fairy tale. But eventually I reached a point where I felt that since the fantasy didn't seem to be withering on the vine I might as well give it a try. My trajectory has not been lucrative. During my years of selling chatchkas in New York City street markets, I usually earned about $4000 a year. But I spent most of my time living in countries where the per capita income is about $120 a year. At thirty, I've never earned more than $12,500 a year, and I am unlikely to make much more for the next five years or so. Yet I can honestly say that in the nine years since I left college, although I've sometimes had money worries, I've never once worried that I would end my days in a dimly lit public housing project.
> *Traveler, anthropologist, former flea market vendor, worked a long time ago for a computer company, thirty*

4. Well-being

When any part of us is neglected (body, mind, or spirit), we are less effective, less happy, and we have less control over our lives. Trust me, I've spent more than one sleepless night in my life watching television, drinking wine, smoking, and eating more pizza and biscuits than you could load onto a truck. That was mostly when I was in law school and then practicing law, which were very far from chasing my dreams. After a night like that, I would be pretty useless. It amazes me to think of how badly I've treated myself at different points in my life and how much I have suffered for it.

If you compare that ridiculous condition with the tremendous benefits of wellness, it seems like a no-brainer: taking good care of your body, mind, and spirit really only requires attention and effort. I don't want to sound like a special health edition of your favorite magazine, but the following are what I have found to be the keys to maintaining a healthy body, mind, and spirit.

Three keys to a healthy body: (1) put healthy food and drink into your body (especially drink a lot of water) and try to limit how much garbage you force your body to process (especially smoke); (2) get plenty of rest; and (3) get some exercise (stretching and walking are easy and very beneficial) every day (morning is best).

Three keys to a healthy mind: (1) do not take yourself too seriously (relax); (2) do take a serious interest in other people, things, events, and issues; and (3) recognize feelings of anxiety so you can learn how to use anxiety without allowing it to paralyze you.

Finally, as hard as I look, I can only find one key to a healthy spirit: just believing in something, anything, and spending some time every day with your true beliefs.

And the ultimate secret to remember for body, mind, and spirit: when you slip up and drag yourself into the gutter for a day, or week, or month, or more, you have to forgive yourself, be patient, and get right back to healthy habits. What else is there to do?

> 66 I could feel like shit or feel great. It's all up to me. Let's see. What will I choose? I'd say it's about fifty/fifty.
>
> *Physician, twenty-nine*

5. Connection with others

Imagine you die (sorry) and your spirit is whisked off to the afterworld. You find yourself in more luxurious circumstances than you ever dreamed of experiencing on Earth. Every conceivable comfort and resource is right at your fingertips. You can have any food, any pleasure, any information, any tools, anything you could possibly desire – for all eternity – except for other people. Are you in heaven or hell?

Human beings have the most compelling need for each other – to be needed, nurtured, understood, and loved. No one has as much power in your life as those whom you love. That's why it's so important to spend time communicating with them. When you actually feel what another person feels, you can often intuit his or her expectations. But, even among the closest people, it is crucial to spell out expectations because disappointed expectations always cause hard feelings. That's why failing to keep commitments is damaging to relationships: when you make a commitment to another person, you are spelling out a set of expectations and then assuming a duty to fulfill those expectations – giving your personal guarantee. Don't give your personal guarantee lightly. If you fail, you will not be lightly forgiven.

> 66 Although I have always worked long hours as a teacher, [at this new school] I was working fourteen to sixteen hours a day and weekends to be prepared for the next day. I did not have an opportunity to spend time with my husband or meet new friends. After much reflection and in-depth discussions with friends and former colleagues. I resigned.
> *School teacher, thirty-one*

6. Growth

If you've ever studied weight training, you know that the way to build muscles is to push them beyond their limits, to the point at which the fibers actually tear, so that they are stronger when they heal. That theory applies to more than just muscles. We only grow when we push ourselves and keep pushing until we feel the pain. Then recover. And then push ourselves some more. Whenever we try to exceed our current level of ability or experience, in any sphere, we move out of our comfort zone into the unknown. We increase the risk of making mistakes and getting hurt.

That's why the key to growth is learning to embrace the unknown, work through mistakes, and tolerate pain. Of course, it would be pointless to venture into the unknown without doing all the research and preparation you can, to risk mistakes without a good backup plan, and to welcome pain that signals injury. But don't turn common sense into an excuse for atrophy. And don't forget that as a living organism you cannot remain static. Atrophy is the only alternative to growth. So push yourself until you feel the pain. Recover. And then push yourself some more.

> **❝** It sounded like a lot of fun. It is sort of an intense physical exhilaration, anticipation, excitement and then once your parachute is open, it is sort of the most incredible feeling. I went the first time out of the excitement of a new experience. The real question is, 'Why did I go back for the second jump?' It was the second one that was really scary because I knew what was coming and I was terrified. The third jump was the first time I really enjoyed it. I could anticipate the excitement and the fear, I could understand what was coming, I could pay more attention to what was happening. That third time, I was in control and when my parachute opened, I was a half mile up near sunset in the fall in New England. This feeling of peace and enjoyment and happiness settled over me. It's a heck of a way to see the leaves.
>
> *On again, off again paralegal, former messenger, part-time*
> *security guard, now studying social psychology, thirty*

■ Daily opportunities to add balance to your life

I hope you will stop saying 'I really should _____' and start acting on your real values and priorities. If you think you don't have time to add balance to your life, you are mistaken. The truth is, you don't have time not to add balance – the more centered, healthy and happy you are, the more productive you'll be. You are surrounded every day by endless opportunities to add balance to your life. Let me suggest a few which seem to work well for many of the people I've interviewed.

Gain control of your creative space

No matter where you work, your ability to assert control over your immediate environment has a huge impact on your sense of well-being. That doesn't mean you must have the corner office (if there is such a thing anymore) with three windows.

Try some of these work space improvements (even if you are working in a cubicle at the outer perimeter of a teaming space) and feel the difference they make in your daily life:

1. Surround yourself with positive visual images: art, photographs, cartoons, portraits, postcards, words, articles, certificates, or something else.

2. Bring aromatherapy into your space: burn scented candles or incense (if you are allowed), bring baked goods or fruit-flavored gum or sweets, wear cologne or perfume or scented lotion that you enjoy, or something aromatic to remind you of your favorite person.

3. Arrange your desk and chair and filing cabinets and tables and bookshelves and bulletin boards and office supplies any way you like them . . . and rearrange them whenever you feel like it.

4. Listen to your favorite CDs or radio station (if you can listen to music without distracting yourself or others).

5. Wear clothing that makes you feel comfortable (if there's

a dress code, then your comfort may have to be limited to the underwear you choose).

6. Bring in your own lamp or lightbulbs for your own preferred lighting – dim, colored, or maybe fluorescent (give the fire code a quick check).

7. Keep at least one inspirational book at easy reach (poetry, philosophy, literature, comedy).

8. Make sure you have enough room to get up and stretch . . . maybe take a little walk, do some push-ups, dance, or something.

9. Don't forget snacks and beverages.

> **"** I surround myself with a lot of personal items. I have a semiprivate work area in the back, but I spend most of my time when the store is open on the floor dealing with customers. That can get really crazy. It really helps to be able to go and spend a few minutes in my own space and collect myself when I need to. I have a book of daily reflections which I read when I want to calm down. It's also just nice to be able to relax for a minute. I have a picture of my family and I can just remind myself why I am working so hard, that it's all worth it.
>
> *Department team leader in a department store, used to work as a retail clerk in a jewelry store, twenty-six*

Give your mind a treat

No matter how intellectually challenging your work may be, your mind cannot survive on a one-track diet. Whether you are fascinated or bored with the subject matter of your work, you need to diversify the sources of your intellectual stimulation. Feed your mind something new every day.

1. If you usually think with your right brain (artistic, emotional, physical), then try thinking with your left brain (logical, mathematical, analytic); and vice versa.

2. Read a novel, or a news magazine, or an encyclopedia of facts.

3. Rent a movie (try something new – if you usually watch mysteries, try a comedy, a thriller, or a foreign film).

4. Write a story, an essay, a poem; sing a song; draw a picture.

5. Work on maths problems or logic problems; do crossword puzzles; play Scrabble or chess.

6. Sit alone and think deeply.

7. Brainstorm out loud with other people.

8. Attend a lecture, play, dance recital, concert, art exhibit or poetry reading.

9. Memorize vocabulary words in a foreign language and practice reading, writing, and speaking.

10. Take a trip to a foreign country.

> **❝** My work is very intellectually challenging, almost to the point of obsession. For a while there I was dreaming about corporate finance. I was doing deal memos in my head. Nobody wanted to talk to me, including me. I couldn't stand what my work was doing to my life and I thought maybe I was really burning out. I tried some different things. I tried reading before bed, but it was really hard to concentrate. My girlfriend was pretty understanding and we would sit and talk, but I couldn't keep from getting all worked up. We tried renting movies in the evening, for a distraction. I even talked to a doctor. What I finally realized was that I couldn't just give myself a pill and get over it. I had to do those kinds of things on a regular basis to get some balance in my life. You have to put limits if you want to have a life.
>
> *Investment banker, thirty-one*

Give your body a treat

Your body, like your mind, benefits from diverse forms of stimulation. That's why cross-training is such a powerful method for achieving physical fitness. But your body, unlike your mind, thrives on routine: sleeping the same hours, eating and drinking familiar mixtures on a regular schedule, performing the same series of stretches and exercises. When you make a big change in your sleeping, eating, or exercise habits, change gradually and with care so it's not too much of a shock to your system. Then try making that change part of a new routine.

1.   Take a walk (thirty minutes every afternoon).

2.   Take a nap (twenty minutes every evening).

3.   Stretch (fifteen minutes every morning).

4.   Do vigorous aerobic activity, like running, biking, hiking, swimming, blading (thirty minutes, four days a week).

5.   Find a teacher and study a physical art, like karate, yoga, tai chi, dance, judo, or rowing (one hour, three days a week).

6.   Play in a sports league (every week).

7.   Drink three liters of water, eat an apple (every day).

8.   Smile, laugh, delight, savor, swoon (whenever possible).

9.   Have sex.

> 66 Initially I was frustrated about living here because there were not a lot of opportunities for me to further my career while my fiancé is finishing veterinary school. But we are on a college campus, which allows us to have a great lifestyle and I have come to enjoy living here. It's really pretty. There is a lake. We go biking and hiking. I am playing soccer at least once or twice a week, year round, and that is a great outlet for me.
> *Working in alumni relations and fundraising, formerly a teaching assistant in a middle school, worked for six months for an investment research organization, twenty-six*

Believe in something

I honestly think that you can cultivate your spiritual side by just believing in something – anything. Before you can believe in anything outside yourself, however, you must first believe in what is inside.

1. Look inside and find out what you already know.

2. Pray.

3. Meditate.

4. Recite affirmations.

5. Read scripture.

6. Read inspirational books, poems, or passages.

7. Listen to inspirational music.

8. Listen to a spiritual adviser, teacher, preacher, or someone else who inspires you.

9. Revel in astonishment at the wonders all around us all the time.

> **"** You have to believe in yourself and believe in other people and do things for the right reasons. That's what I believe. And I remind myself of that every single day. If I am going to be the best person I can be, I have to treat people fairly and always try to do things for the right reasons. It all comes back to you.
>
> *Owner of a Dairy Queen restaurant where he worked behind the counter as a teenager (has balanced bank loans, construction jobs, and even paper rounds to get the business on its feet), also currently working full-time as an executive recruiter, twenty-nine*

Spend time with people you care about

The only way to get close to people and stay close with them is by giving them your undivided attention at least some of the time. If you are lucky enough to be in love, to be a parent, to have parents, to have a best friend, siblings, or cousins, spend some time with them.

1. Invite your new friends over for dinner.

2. Volunteer at a soup kitchen with your kids.

3. Read a book to your niece.

4. Write a letter to your nephew.

5. Send an e-mail to your best friend.

6. Go home to visit your parents.

7. Talk on the phone with your siblings.

8. Take a long walk with your lover.

9. Take your whole family on vacation.

> ❝ Choosing a law school was a pivotal decision for me in a way that I could not have predicted. I had it in mind that I wanted to go to Harvard or Yale – that had always been a big goal for me. I got into Columbia early on in the process and my mother encouraged me to go to Columbia – it's a great school and it was much closer to home. From a retrospective point of view, I am very glad I went to school that close to home. It meant that I got to spend a lot more time with my mum. That turned out to be really important to me because my mum passed away unexpectedly just a couple of years ago. I am very glad we had that time together.
>
> *Lawyer (working at third law firm in five years), community leader, with a small music production company on the side, also advises entrepreneurs, twenty-nine*

Gain control of your time

It's a lot easier to work cheerfully and effectively (whether it's twenty hours a week or one hundred) when you have the power to decide when you are going to eat, sleep, relax, work out, and spend time with people you care about. Take advantage of some of the flexible schedule arrangements that more and more employers are making available to their employees.

1. Manage your own time so well (never miss deadlines) that your managers won't even think of trying to manage it for you.

2. 'Just say no' when anyone tries to give you tasks and responsibilities that you don't have time to accomplish.

3. 'Just do it' when you are in need of a morning stroll, an afternoon nap, a day off, or a vacation.

4. Volunteer for a compressed schedule (forty hours in four days).

5. Consider scaling back a full-time job to part-time.

6. Take a sabbatical from work (tell them you don't want to quit, but you'd like six months off).

7. Consider sharing one full-time job between yourself and another person.

8. If the tasks you perform don't need to be done at any particular time of day, try getting on a flexitime schedule – start your work week at 6.00 a.m. on Wednesday, noon on Saturday, or midnight Sunday.

9. Set up a home office and make arrangements for telecommuting.

> **❝** I have an idea about pursuing a career in human resources, but I just had a baby, and I am trying to figure out how to do everything. I have this idea about how it could work. See, I am overqualified in one way – I have a lot of experience and skill in recruiting, hiring, orientation, training, and integrating people into a corporate culture. But I am underqualified in that I don't have the training on the financial side – compensation and benefits. I have thought about being entrepreneurial and recruiting the other half of the ticket, someone who knows compensation and benefits, then we could market ourselves together as a package and share the job. That way I could solve all my problems at once. I would have a job with the kind of hours I want, would be working in an area where I want to work, could learn the comp and benefits aspects

of the job over time from my job partner, and would gladly sacrifice half the money for a deal like that – more than half. Why have someone killing herself in a job, or just not able to do a job, when you could have two people working happily and comfortably together in a way that works for their lives?

Worked as recruiting and human resources director at a large law firm for several years, then for two years at another firm, in between worked part-time at another firm, recently moved again, twenty-nine

Building yourself requires as much time, energy, creativity and focus as building your career. You cannot build a powerhouse career unless you are building a powerhouse you at the same time. As you get in touch with your personal priorities, maximize every opportunity to live by them and keep moving toward a balanced center.

Take it one year at a time

In a rapidly changing world defined by chaos and uncertainty, long-term goals are merely useful hallucinations.

> ❝ I've been running a Dairy Queen since I was 22. And I've wondered, 'What am I going to do if I sell the store?' So right now, I am working as a headhunter in the pharmaceutical industry. As a headhunter, I am constantly looking at all these available jobs and so I am looking at new options for myself every day. Right now, my wife is running the Dairy Queen and we're training a guy who we hope will buy us out in about eight years. Of course, ten year goals change every year which means you have to keep adjusting your plan. But, that's OK, its not like I am putting all my eggs in one basket and it sure seems like we are moving in the right direction.
>
> *Owner of the now fully renovated and expanded Dairy Queen restaurant where he worked behind the counter as a teenager, balancing bank loans, construction jobs, and even paper rounds to get the business on its feet, currently working as an executive recruiter, twenty-nine*

> ❝ If you don't make stuff happen, stuff just starts happening to you.
>
> *College senior, juggling part-time jobs and placements, twenty-two*

> ❝ It seems like, no matter how hard you try to plan, things never quite work out the way you think they will. But, it still seems like a good idea to plan. I guess you plan, go according to plan for a while, until you realize that you have to change your plan and then you go for a while until you have to change your plan again.
>
> *First-year graduate student in forestry after two years of balancing placements, retail jobs, and graduate courses, twenty-four*

> ❝ The company [where I worked] had changed; it just wasn't the same company. This made me think about the long term, something I hadn't done before, and I realized that [this company] was not where I wanted to be. I lacked a

clear direction and vision. I probably should have widened my sights and looked into other possibilities. Who knows what great opportunities were passed up? Being successful in the chosen path does not mean that path was necessarily the best one to take.

Former electrical engineer, now a patent lawyer, practiced law for nine months at a major law firm, now working as a judicial clerk, thirty

❝ Point and shoot. That's the way I plan. Plan for one second, and then do it. If it doesn't work, get the ball, and do it again.

Analyst in an accounting/consulting firm, formerly working several part-time jobs to pay for school, thinking about going back to graduate school for an MBA, twenty-five

❝ Looking back, I realize that no experience has been a waste. Each experience has moved me further toward today and I love where I am today.

Book store assistant, part-time entrepreneur, poet, chess teacher, formerly assistant manager at Wendy's Burgers, at one time destitute, collecting welfare, and living in a homeless shelter, thirty-two

❝ My parents are always telling me I should have my whole life planned out. If I did that, I'd have to redo it every year. I know what I want right now and I know how to get it. I keep my plans up to date with what I need to get out of life.

Painting houses, doing odd jobs, waiting tables, playing guitar in a band, living with parents but planning to move to 'a big city,' twenty-three

❝ I entered grad school figuring that there was about a fifty/fifty chance that I'd stick with it, but that at least I should find out for myself rather than just leaving it as an unfulfilled fantasy. I could never have gotten to where I am today if I hadn't been an inveterate procrastinator since kindergarten (I used to pull all-nighters for book reports, no kidding). Also, that all those teachers who kept telling me that tardiness would stop working as a strategy 'next year' were, of course, wrong. [But] I'd never recommend the kind of haphazard life strategy I've chosen. It would be far too anxiety producing.

Anthropology graduate student, traveler, former flea market entrepreneur, thirty

From long-term hallucinations to effective one year planning

Most five and ten year goals, set today, have virtually no chance of ever materializing. How could they? In five or ten years, we will be spending the majority of our time doing things that haven't even been thought of yet. But don't be paralyzed. Don't let uncertainty keep you from making detailed plans and acting on them vigorously every single day. A long-term goal is like a mirage in the desert: you move perpetually towards that oasis. Your destination changes constantly and you will probably never arrive. Even though it is a hallucination, your long-term vision is useful if it keeps moving you in the right direction by helping you set realistic and concrete one year goals. One year goals will be the centerpiece of your one year plan.

Start with your long-term vision/ hallucination of your future

Do you have a clear long-term vision? What does your life and career look like in fifteen or twenty years? Picture your ideal vision:

What have you learned? And, what are you learning?

▷   Are you an expert in a particular field? Law? Medicine? Computers? Football? Art? Literature? Science?

▷   Are you well educated? Self-taught? Do people come to you for advice?

▷   Are you considered 'the best' at something?

▷   Are you still practicing, learning, thinking,
    studying?

With whom have you built relationships? And with whom are you building relationships?

▷   Are you closest to your family, friends, and
    spouse/lover?
▷   Who are your colleagues? Clients, customers? Who
    do you do business with?
▷   Who are your mentors? Protégés?
▷   Are you still cultivating relationships with people
    you care about?

Where have you added value? And how are you adding value?

▷   Have you been working for yourself, or for
    someone else? As a professional? As a volunteer?
    As a valued team player? As a lone entrepreneur?
▷   Have you discovered a problem no one else
    discovered?
▷   Have you solved a problem no one else has solved?
▷   Have you improved a product or service? Or
    invented something new?
▷   Are you still contributing to the world around you?

How have you kept your life in balance? And how are you keeping your life in balance?

▷   Do you have a gratifying home life? Are you close
    to the people who matter to you in your life?
▷   Have you lived your life with integrity? Are you
    proud of what you have produced in your life?
    Have you sought after your dreams? Are you
    content?
▷   Are you healthy – in mind, body, and spirit? Are
    you an athlete? Do you work out? Do you read?
    Meditate?

▪ Are you a balanced, centered person, upon whom others can depend?

As you go through the long-term vision exercise, please remember: I am encouraging you to hallucinate about the future and hallucinations can be very distracting. Sometimes we get so caught up in our long-term visions that we don't have enough presence of mind to start making them come true. Use your long-term vision as a mirage – an oasis off in the distance to keep moving toward. Now, let's concentrate on moving in the right direction in the coming year, month, week, tomorrow, and today.

▪ Make a one year plan

There are five steps in the process of making an effective one year plan.

Step 1

Set one year goals for learning, relationships, adding value, and moving your life toward balance. What concrete goals can you realistically achieve in each category in the next year?

Step 2

Map out all the intermediate goals and deadlines along the way to each one year goal. If you are going to achieve your one year goals, what must you achieve by the eleven month mark? Ten? Nine, eight, seven, six, five, four, three, two, and one? Spend time mapping out all the intermediate goals and deadlines to keep you on track toward your one year goals.

Step 3

Take time at the beginning of every month to carve up the achievement of intermediate goals into bite-size chunks that can be accomplished in less than a day. At the beginning of each month, map out all the daily actions necessary to achieve each of your intermediate goals.

Step 4

Schedule your time effectively to plan all the daily actions necessary to achieve your goals. Schedule your time effectively and plan every week exactly *when* you are going take the actions necessary to achieve your goals. There is a lot of time in a week. It's worth planning that time. Spend some time at the beginning of each week to review all of your upcoming intermediate deadlines and the daily actions which must be achieved to meet those deadlines. Plan your time carefully each week and plug those daily actions into your weekly schedule.

There are 168 hours in every single week. Most people sleep less than 56 hours a week, leaving 112 hours. How many hours do you need to relax, work out, eat, shower, and whatever? Be generous . . . 32 hours each week? That leaves 80 hours a week. Let's say you work 40 hours a week and commute 10. That still leaves you with 30 hours every single week to do . . . whatever you decide to do.

Step 5

Monitor feedback from the world around you and continue making necessary adjustments in your goals and plans every step of the way. When following an action plan in a climate of rapid change, you must be very sensitive to feedback from the world around you. What is changing? What is staying the same? What is working? What is no longer working? As circumstances change, you'll need to be flexible enough to adjust your goals. As you discover which strategies and techniques are working and which are not, you'll need to recalibrate yourself and fine-tune your actions. As long as you keep adjusting your goals, planning, and taking deliberate action, day by day, you'll keep moving forward: learning, building relationships, tackling creative challenges, and keeping your life in balance. That's how you'll keep growing from within, building yourself, inventing your career, and reinventing success and security.

Epilog

Every new generation of workers faces historically specific challenges in starting out its careers. But our generation is entering the workforce during the most profound changes in the economy since the Industrial Revolution. As the very nature of work changes radically, so do the dynamics of managing a successful career. Those twin realities are a little unnerving for some people – I hope that after reading this book you will find them rather exhilarating.

Inventing your career in the workplace of the future will be challenging, no doubt. In order to succeed, you'll have to work hard and work smart. And there probably won't ever be a pinnacle on which you can rest for too long, no matter how much success you accumulate. The world today is just too fast-paced and competitive for any of us to rest on our laurels . . . ever.

This truth, and everything else I've shared in this book, I have learned over the last four years by interviewing more than a thousand young people who are struggling and succeeding in the post-jobs economy. I've also learned a tremendous amount from ditching my own career as a lawyer at a major New York law firm to start Rainmaker. And I've learned just as much from the experiences of the other people who have worked with us here at Rainmaker.

When I quit my job at the law firm, I was taking a giant leap of faith in my own ability to design the kind of life and career I wanted for myself because I didn't really know what kind of life and career I wanted. I was in the middle of writing my first book, *Managing Generation X*, but 'working on a book' didn't feel like much of a career, especially since I wasn't sure if I'd be able to get it published.

I moved to Connecticut because that was where my wife Debby Applegate was going to graduate school. We had been stretching ourselves between Debby's dorm room in New Haven and our apartment in New York City. We were relieved at the chance to consolidate our life, at least for a while, and we moved all of our stuff into an inexpensive three bedroom apartment in New Haven. While Debby continued grad school, I gave birth to Rainmaker.

When I first approached my old friend Jeff Coombs about becoming the other managing principal of Rainmaker, I didn't have a detailed plan for how Rainmaker could be a viable source of income for either of us. I did know I hated being a lawyer, and I had a feeling that I didn't want to just get another 'job.' For his part, Jeff knew he didn't want to keep working as a computer software trainer and he didn't want to go back to being a systems consultant, his first job out of college. The one thing of which we were both sure was that we wanted to take control of our own careers and work for ourselves instead of working for someone else.

One thing I knew I could do to make money was manage political campaigns (something I had done before). I had been studying the latest in high-tech campaign strategy, trying to design the 'perfect' campaign. Jeff had the sophisticated computer skills I was missing. By the summer of 1994, we were in business for ourselves. After working side by side fifteen hours a day, seven days a week, for months on end on a state senate campaign in Connecticut, Jeff and I knew that we made a great team. But after the election we realized that we had no money, no clients, and not much of a plan.

Jeff had moved to New Haven and was living in the same third floor walk-up with Debby and me as none of us could afford to live on our own. The business we wanted to start – a think tank to study our generation in the workplace – didn't seem like the kind of business that would start making money overnight. It sure didn't feel like a very lucrative project when we were huddled under jackets in our freezing cold apartment, trying to sound businesslike over the phone.

By spring 1995, we had moved Rainmaker out of the extra bedroom and into the vacant apartment on the first floor of the same building. By summer, Rainmaker had two new recruits: my childhood friend Jeff Katz and the friend of a friend from college, Homer Robinson.

Quitting his job and moving to New Haven was a big decision for Jeff Katz because he had a wife and a three-year-old son to consider. But the Katz's had been on the move for several years already: during his first year out of college, Jeff worked in real estate in Philadelphia for the father of one of his college friends. The next year, Jeff took a job in the foreign service and the Katzes lived in Washington until they were stationed on the other side of the planet – in Malaysia, where they lived for three years. When they returned to Washington, Jeff started feeling dissatisfied with his government job and decided to take me up on my standing offer to join Rainmaker. Jeff spent a year with us, trying to decide whether he wanted to be an entrepreneur, apply to law school, or do something altogether different. He went to work for a local business association, whose director Jeff had gotten to know through his work at Rainmaker. Now he's in law school.

Homer Robinson came to us from circumstances very different from the Jeff Katz scenario, but also very much the same: Homer was unmarried, had no kids, no real obligations, nothing whatsoever to tie him down. Far from having been tied down, Homer had been on the move, traveling all over Eastern Europe, even working for a while as a journalist when he lived in Bulgaria. Then he worked for a year as a journalist in New Mexico before returning to his home town of New York City. By the time Homer came to us, he was looking for direction. We couldn't afford to pay him, but I offered Homer the spare bedroom in the upstairs apartment, which he accepted – so now Debby and I had two roommates. For six months, Homer was a one-man public relations army, booking hundreds of interviews and placing stories in newspapers, magazines, and on radio and television. And then wanderlust struck again and Homer went off to Africa as an apprentice cameraman on a safari film.

Rainmaker's ranks have crested and swelled several times. Since January 1995, we have employed twenty-five different people – for as long as two years and as short a time as two weeks. Maybe it sounds like we have a hard time retaining employees here at Rainmaker. The truth is that Rainmaker is a prototype of the post-jobs company: our growth is driven by a steady stream of day-to-day value adders – each learning, growing, and making important contributions to the company before moving on to another new experience. Those who don't move on are continually reinventing themselves and their roles in the company. It may be a new way to grow a company, but we are growing at a rate of 800 percent annually.

As we try to keep up with Rainmaker's growth, we are fortunate to have the tremendous contributions of a steady stream of short-term value adders as well as a solid core group.

When Heather Boardman came to work for us fresh out of college, she was frustrated with her inability to find work in her field of study (counseling). Heather wasn't sure who we were or what we were doing and she didn't have much experience as an office administrator – but she figured working here would be a great opportunity to learn new skills and work in an easygoing environment. Now she's practically running the place.

Mark Kurber is a natural born entrepreneur – I've known him since I was a little kid. When I described what we were doing here, Mark offered to sell our seminars on a strictly commission basis. He was so confident of his ability to add value, he was willing to take all the risk. Now he is on salary, working as Rainmaker's in-house entrepreneur.

Our newest addition, Ruth Gutman, has just completed a prolonged college experience. She's not going to be using her farm-hand experience much at Rainmaker, but her command of French may come in handy.

As my wife Debby finishes her Ph.D. at Yale, she is discovering the overwhelming odds of the academic job market, where thousands of highly qualified applicants scramble for a handful of job openings each year. Hustling for crumbs in the ivory tower is leading Debby to consider career options outside of academics.

We are still living upstairs on the third floor – over the store, as it were. And Jeff and I are still building what *USA Today* calls 'that funky think tank Rainmaker.' I'm still not sure how 'funky' we are, but we are building a post-jobs company in a new kind of industry – what many call 'the knowledge industry' but which I prefer to call 'the meaning industry.' We are having fun, supporting our research and supporting ourselves. Each of us has designed our own life and career exactly the way we want it and we are living it.

As you invent the life and career you want for yourself, you are certain to encounter many challenges. Don't let those challenges scare you back to the land of the old-fashioned career path. That path leads nowhere. Take a giant leap of faith in yourself – in your own skills and abilities, your own strength of purpose, your own diligence, your own persistence. Refuse to fail. Insist on success – on your own terms and nobody else's. It is my deepest hope that this book has helped you and will continue to help you in that effort.

Index